ANGEL™

LONG NIGHT'S JOURNEY

Based on the TV series created by
Joss Whedon & David Greenwalt

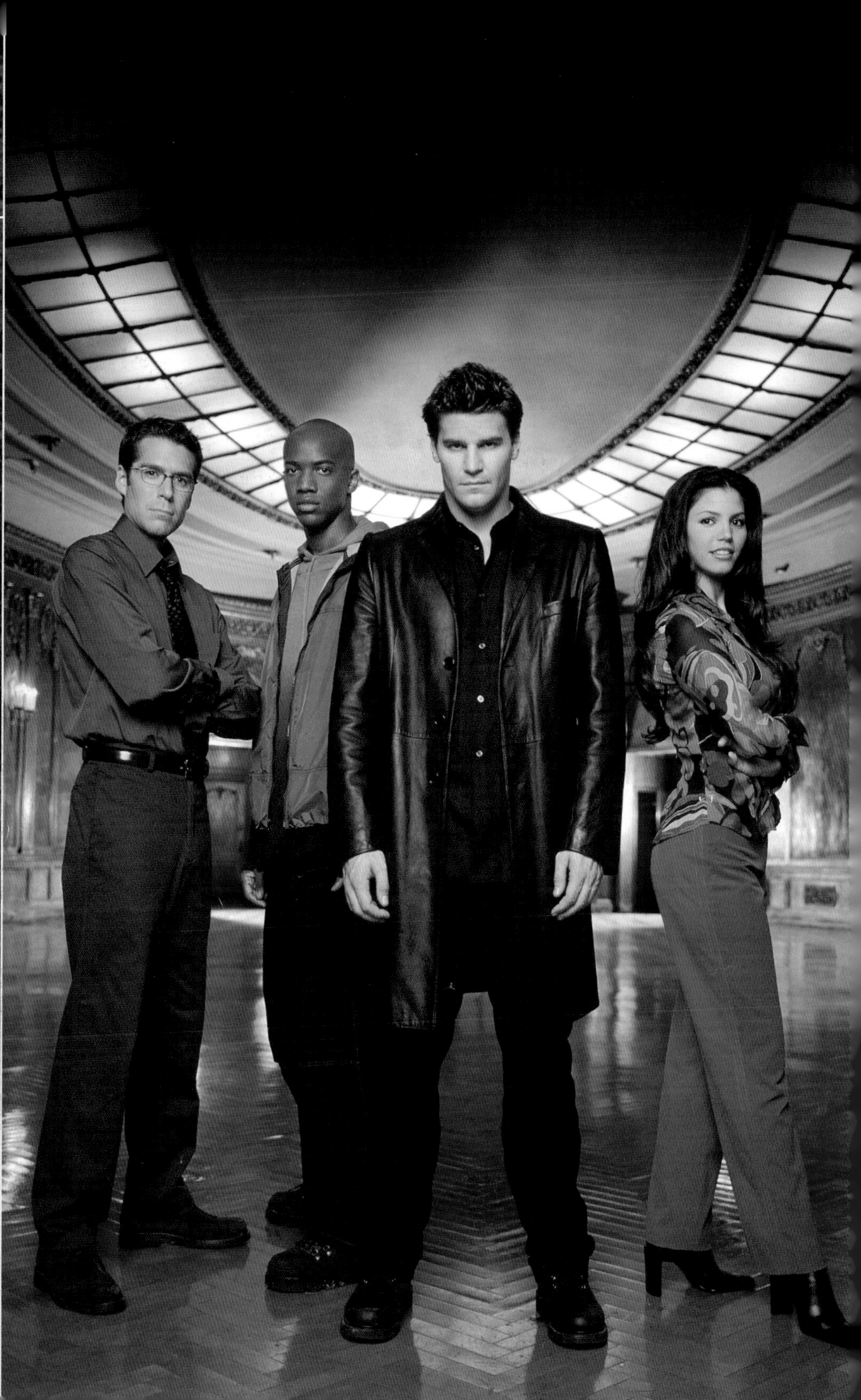

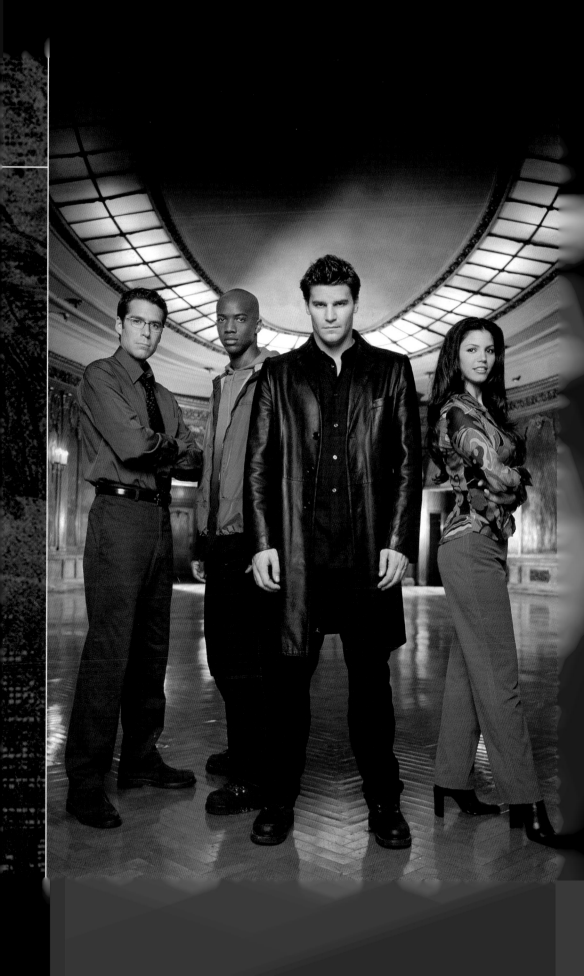

ANGEL™

LONG NIGHT'S JOURNEY

story
Brett Matthews and Joss Whedon

pencils
Mel Rubi

inks
Chris Dreier

letters
Pat Brosseau

colors
Michelle Madsen and Dave Stewart
and Digital Chameleon

dedicated to
J.D. Peralta

publisher
MIKE RICHARDSON

editor
SCOTT ALLIE
with MIKE CARRIGLITTO

collection designer
DEBRA BAILEY

art director
MARK COX

Special thanks to
DEBBIE OLSHAN at Fox Licensing.

Published by
Dark Horse Comics, Inc.
10956 SE Main Street
Milwaukie, OR 97222

First edition: June 2002
ISBN: 1-56971-752-4

1 3 5 7 9 10 8 6 4 2

Printed in China.

This story takes place during Angel's second season. This book collects
issues one through four of the Dark Horse comic book series, Angel.

One

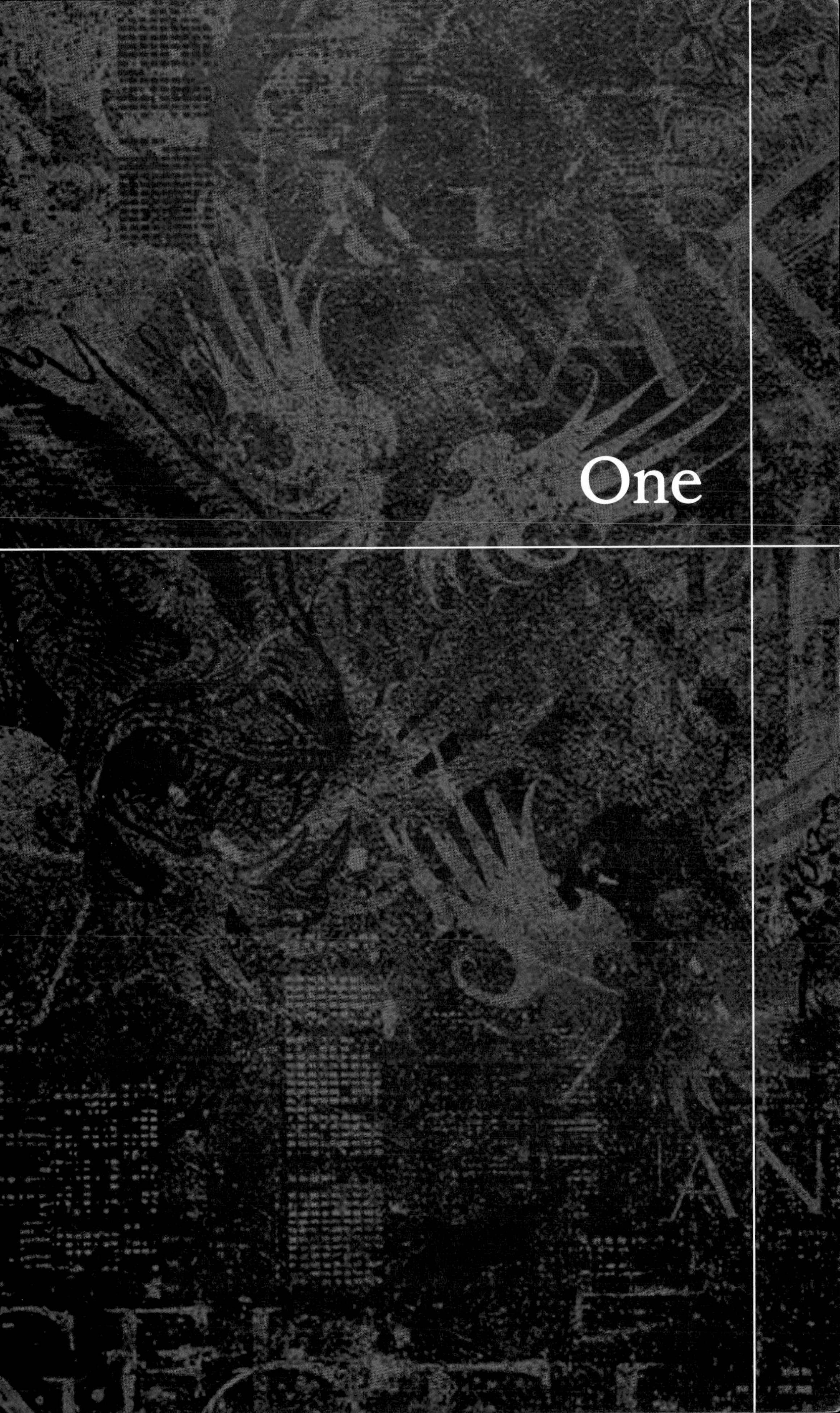

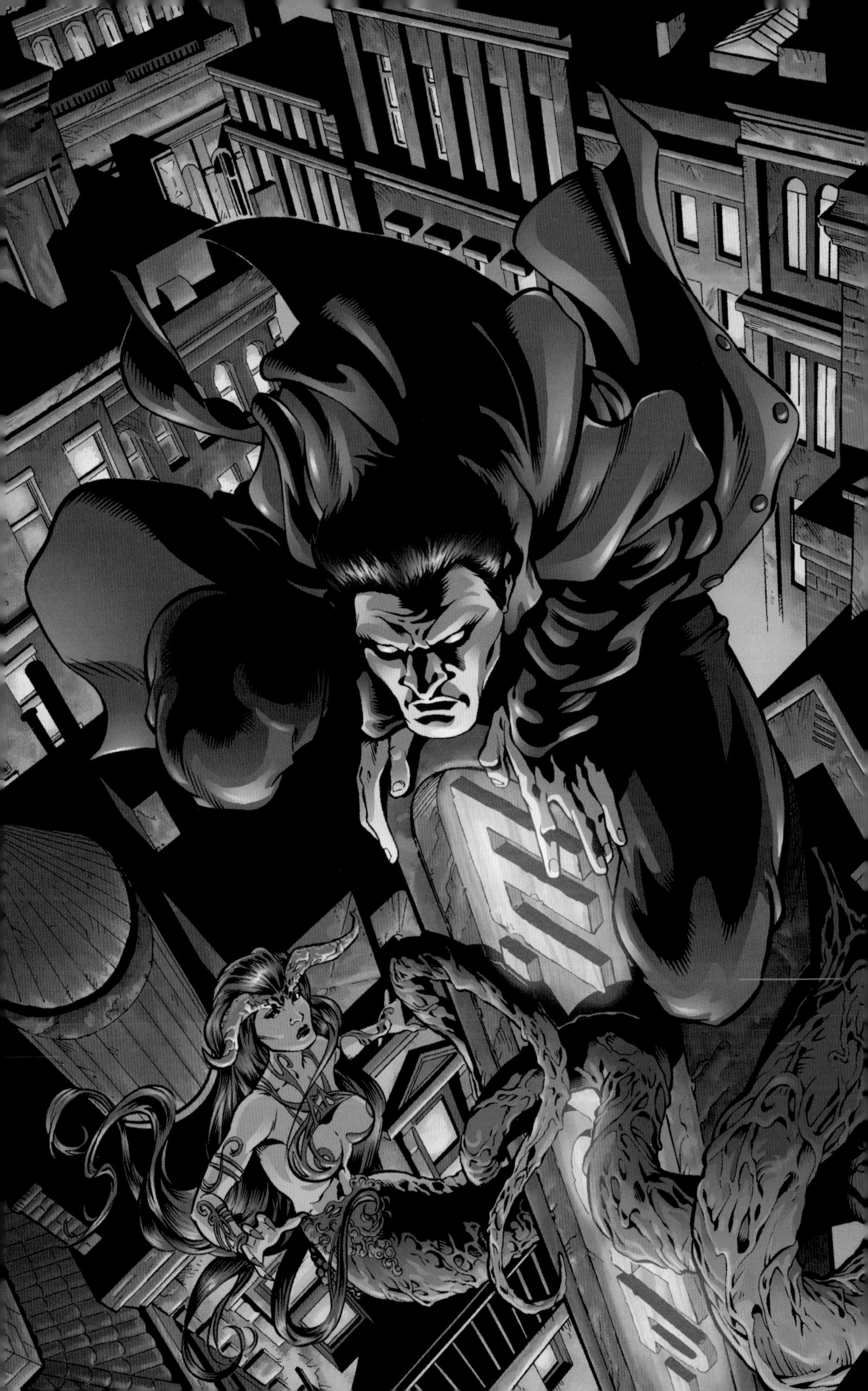

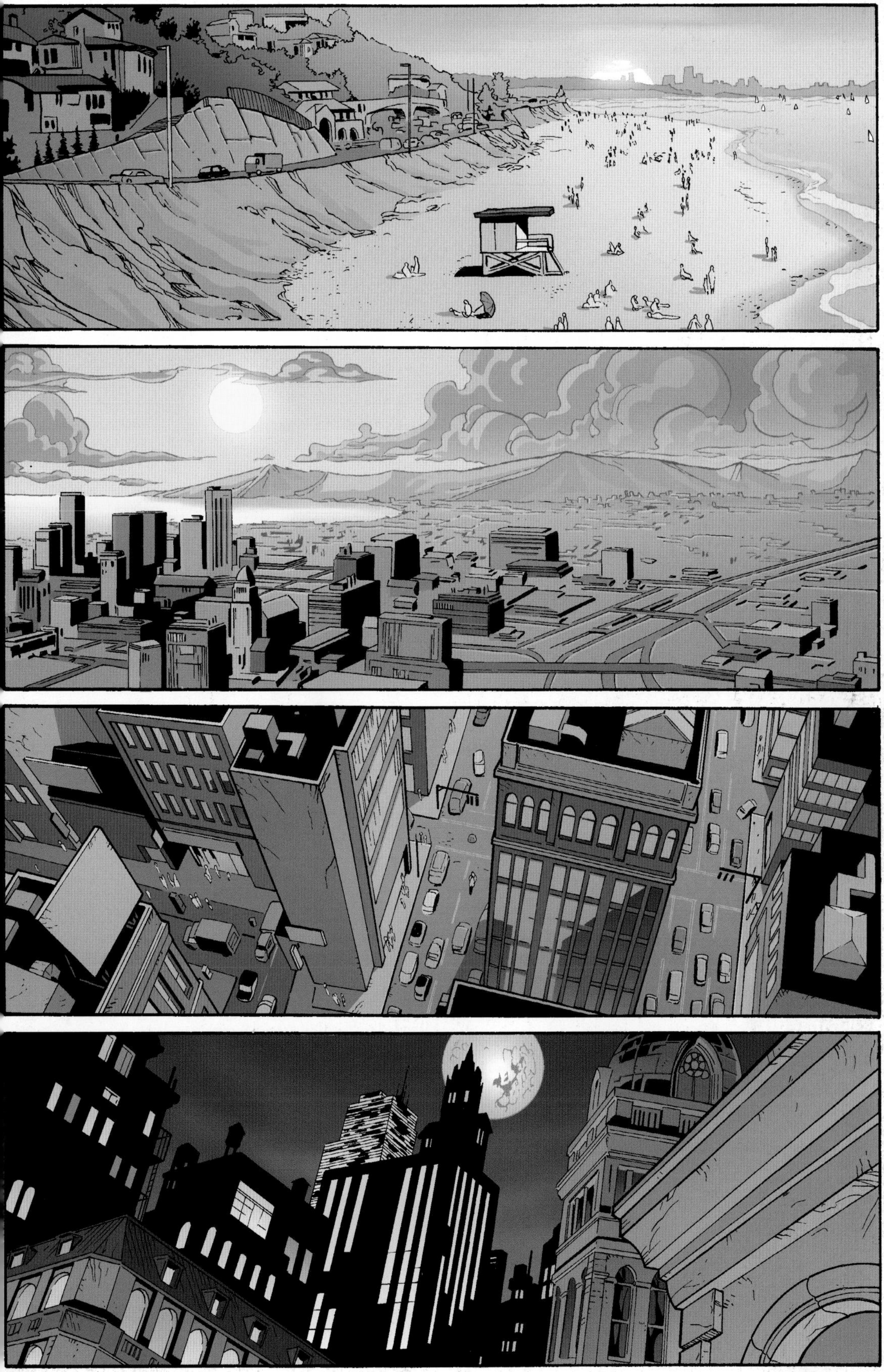

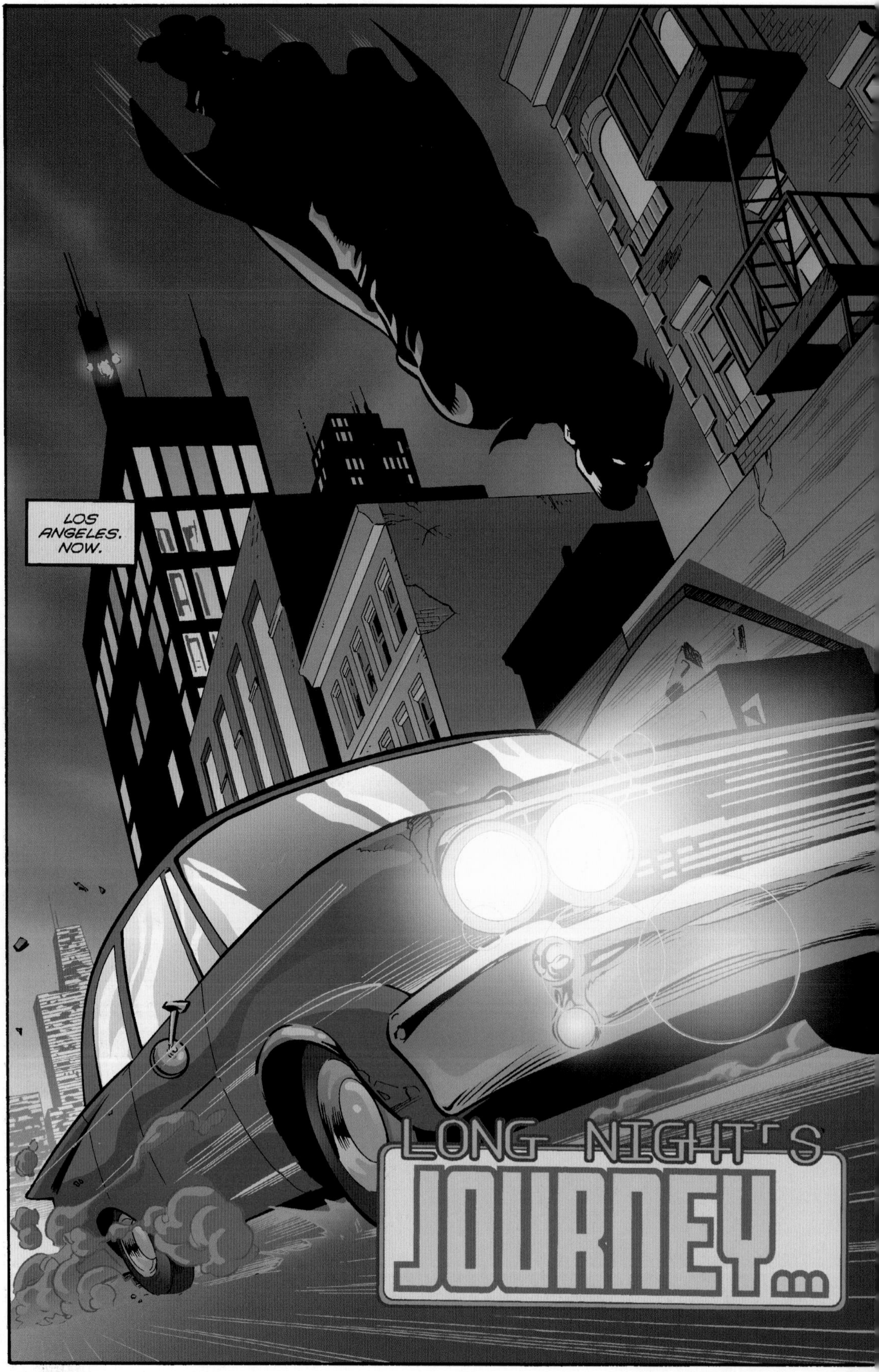
LOS ANGELES. NOW.
LONG NIGHT'S
JOURNEY...

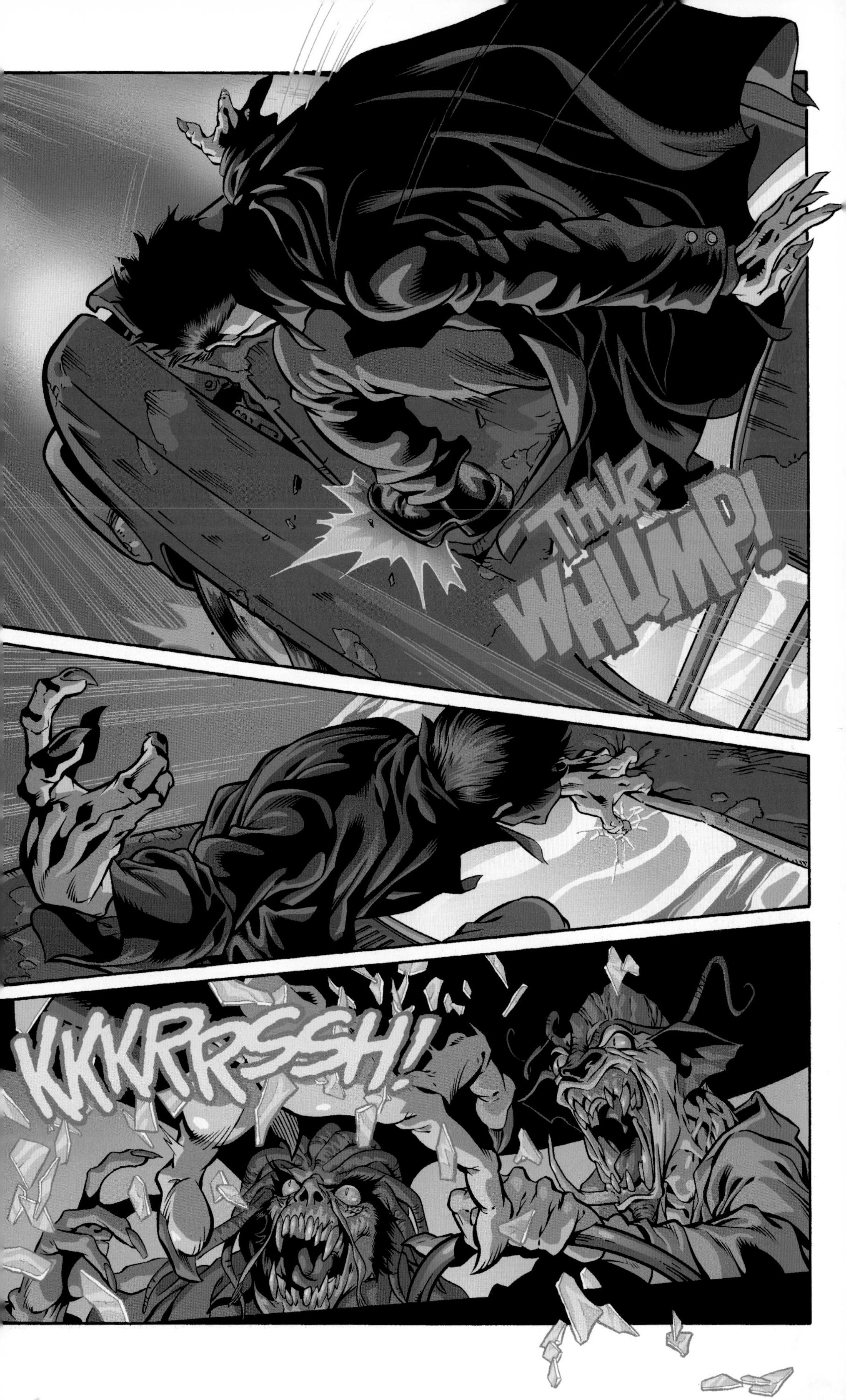
THUR-
WHUMP!
KKKRRSSH!

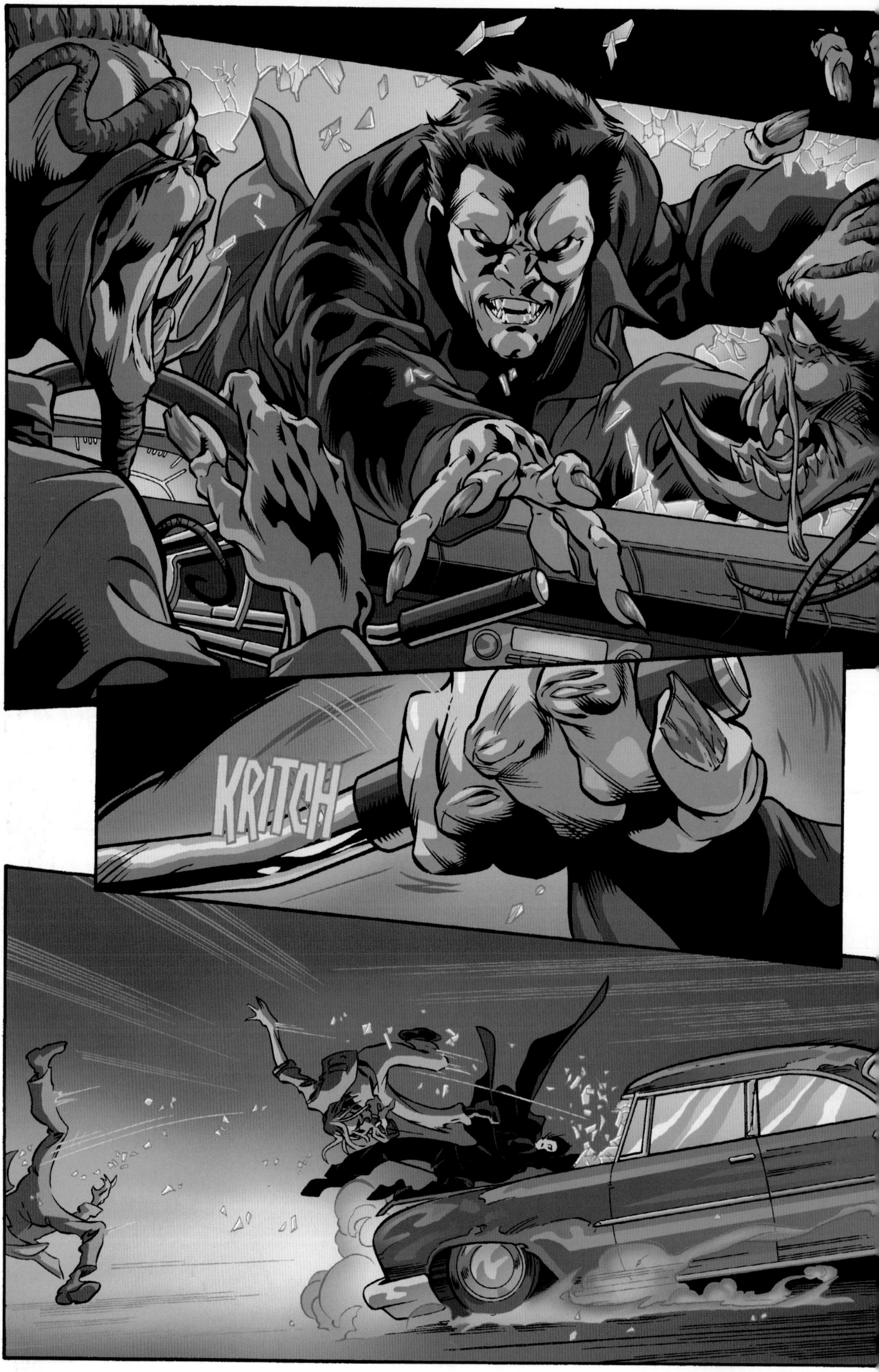
KRITCH

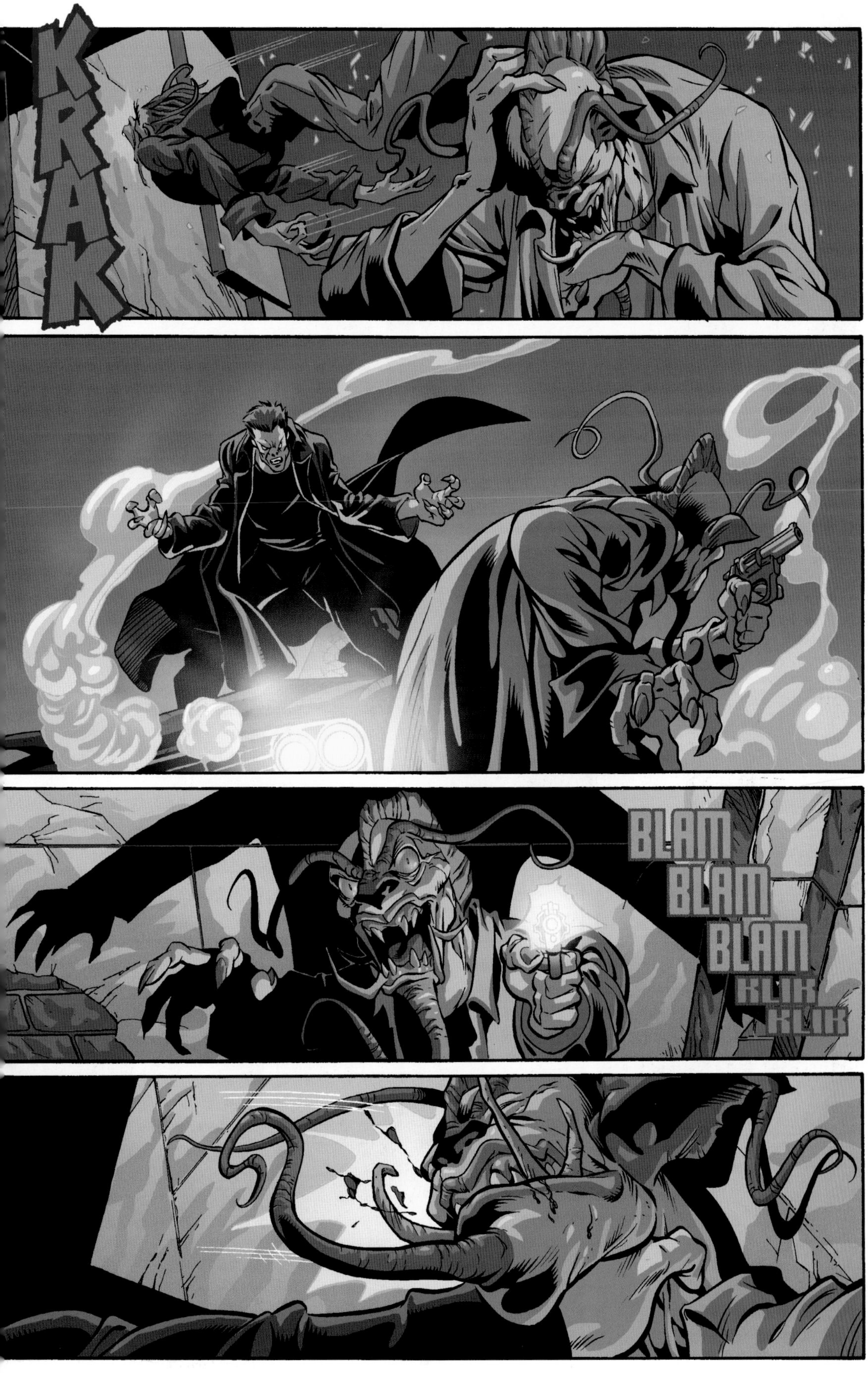
KRAK
BLAM
BLAM
BLAM
KLIK
KLIK

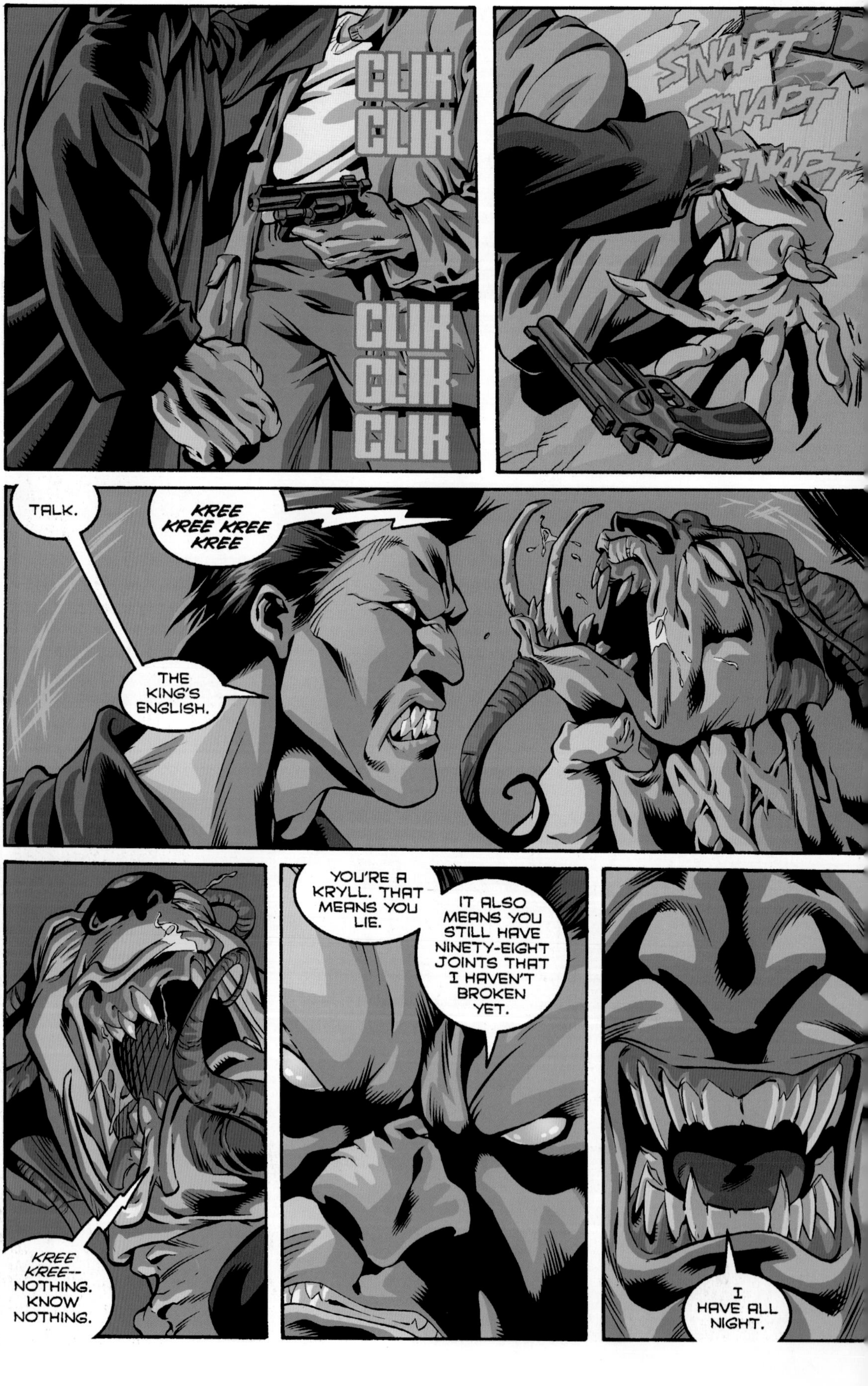
CLIK
CLIK
CLIK
CLIK
CLIK
SNAPT
SNAPT
SNAPT
TALK.
KREE KREE KREE KREE
THE KING'S ENGLISH.
KREE KREE-- NOTHING. KNOW NOTHING.
YOU'RE A KRYLL. THAT MEANS YOU LIE.
IT ALSO MEANS YOU STILL HAVE NINETY-EIGHT JOINTS THAT I HAVEN'T BROKEN YET.
I HAVE ALL NIGHT.

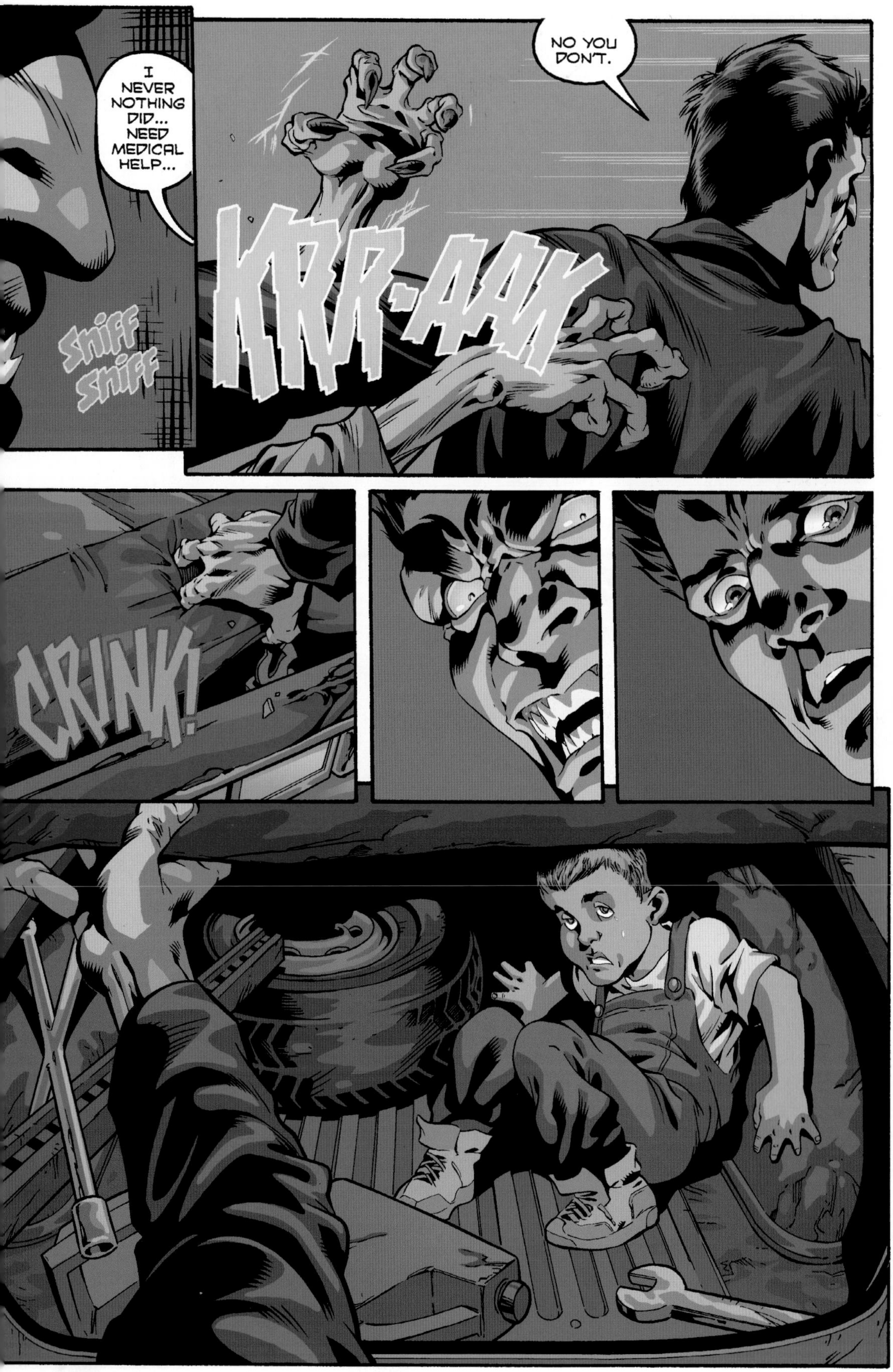

I NEVER NOTHING DID... NEED MEDICAL HELP...
SNIFF SNIFF
NO YOU DON'T.
KRR-AAK
CRINK!

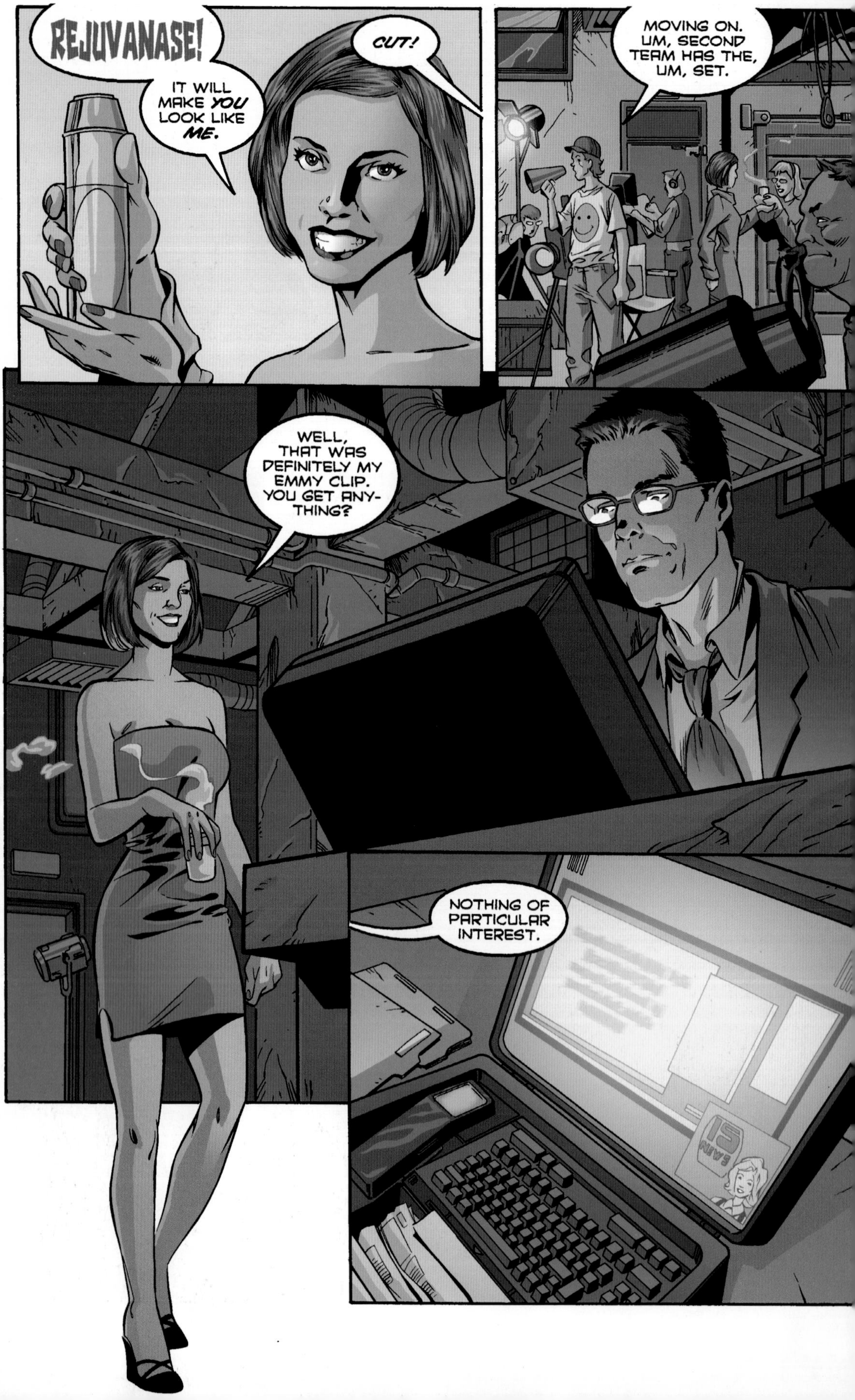
REJUVANASE!
IT WILL MAKE YOU LOOK LIKE ME.
CUT!
MOVING ON. UM, SECOND TEAM HAS THE, UM, SET.
WELL, THAT WAS DEFINITELY MY EMMY CLIP. YOU GET ANY-THING?
NOTHING OF PARTICULAR INTEREST.
15 NEWS

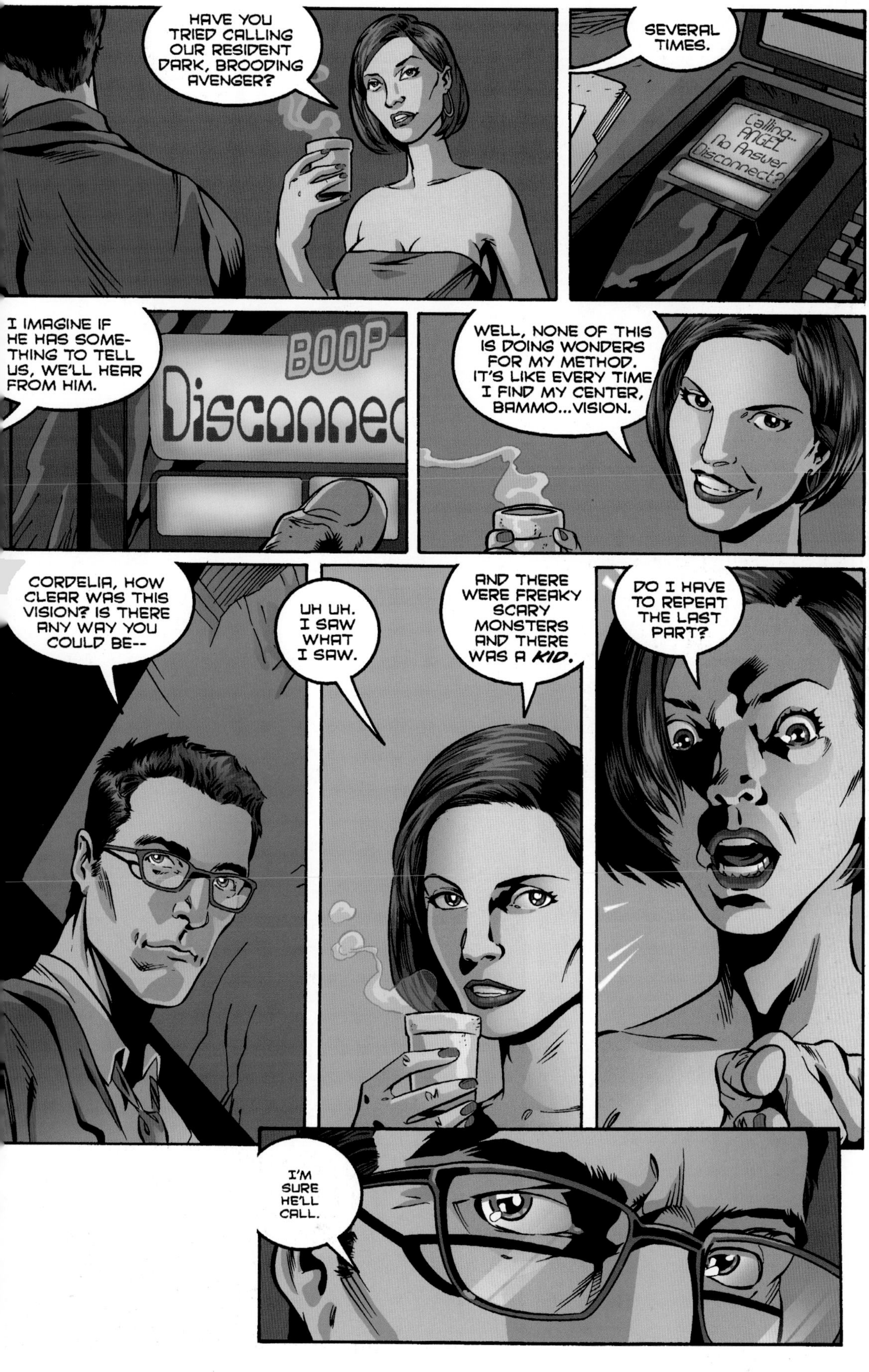
HAVE YOU TRIED CALLING OUR RESIDENT DARK, BROODING AVENGER?
SEVERAL TIMES.
Calling... ANGEL No Answer Disconnect?
I IMAGINE IF HE HAS SOMETHING TO TELL US, WE'LL HEAR FROM HIM.
BOOP
Disconnec
WELL, NONE OF THIS IS DOING WONDERS FOR MY METHOD. IT'S LIKE EVERY TIME I FIND MY CENTER, BAMMO...VISION.
CORDELIA, HOW CLEAR WAS THIS VISION? IS THERE ANY WAY YOU COULD BE--
UH UH. I SAW WHAT I SAW.
AND THERE WERE FREAKY SCARY MONSTERS AND THERE WAS A KID.
DO I HAVE TO REPEAT THE LAST PART?
I'M SURE HE'LL CALL.

I DON'T KNOW WHAT HIS PROBLEM WITH CELL-PHONES IS. I MEAN HE'S SEEN EVERYTHING, 150 YEARS OF PROGRESS AND *CELLPHONES* FREAK HIM OUT? *ZEPPELINS,* OKAY, WEIRD--BUT CELL-PHONES? SMALL AND CUTE AND USEFUL AND HE SHOULD JUST GET OVER IT.

CORDELIA--

I JUST WANT SOME CLOSURE, OKAY? I WANT THAT KID SAFE AND THIS SHOOT OVER SO I CAN RELAX AND WHAT THE HELL IS *REJUVANASE* ANYWAY? LIKE ANY OVER-THE-COUNTER GOOP IS GONNA MAKE SARAH PLAIN & TALL LOOK LIKE *THIS.*

CORDELIA--

AND YOU KNOW WHAT'S ALSO A GOOD IDEA SAVORING COFFEE WHERE IN ACTUAL COFFEE BEANS HAVE TOUCHED THE WATER AT SOME POINT, HELPS GIVE IT THAT *COFFEE* LIKE FLAVOR, WHEN I'M DISGUSTINGLY FAMOUS I'M GONNA HAVE A CAPPUCCINO MACHINE IN EVERY--

CORDELIA!

WHAT?

JUST MAKE SURE YOU REMEMBER TO BREATHE.

WELL SEEING AS I'M THE ONLY ONE THROWING IDEAS OUT HERE, YOU TRIED CALLING OUR *OTHER* DARK, BROODING AVENGER?

ONE STEP AHEAD OF YOU.

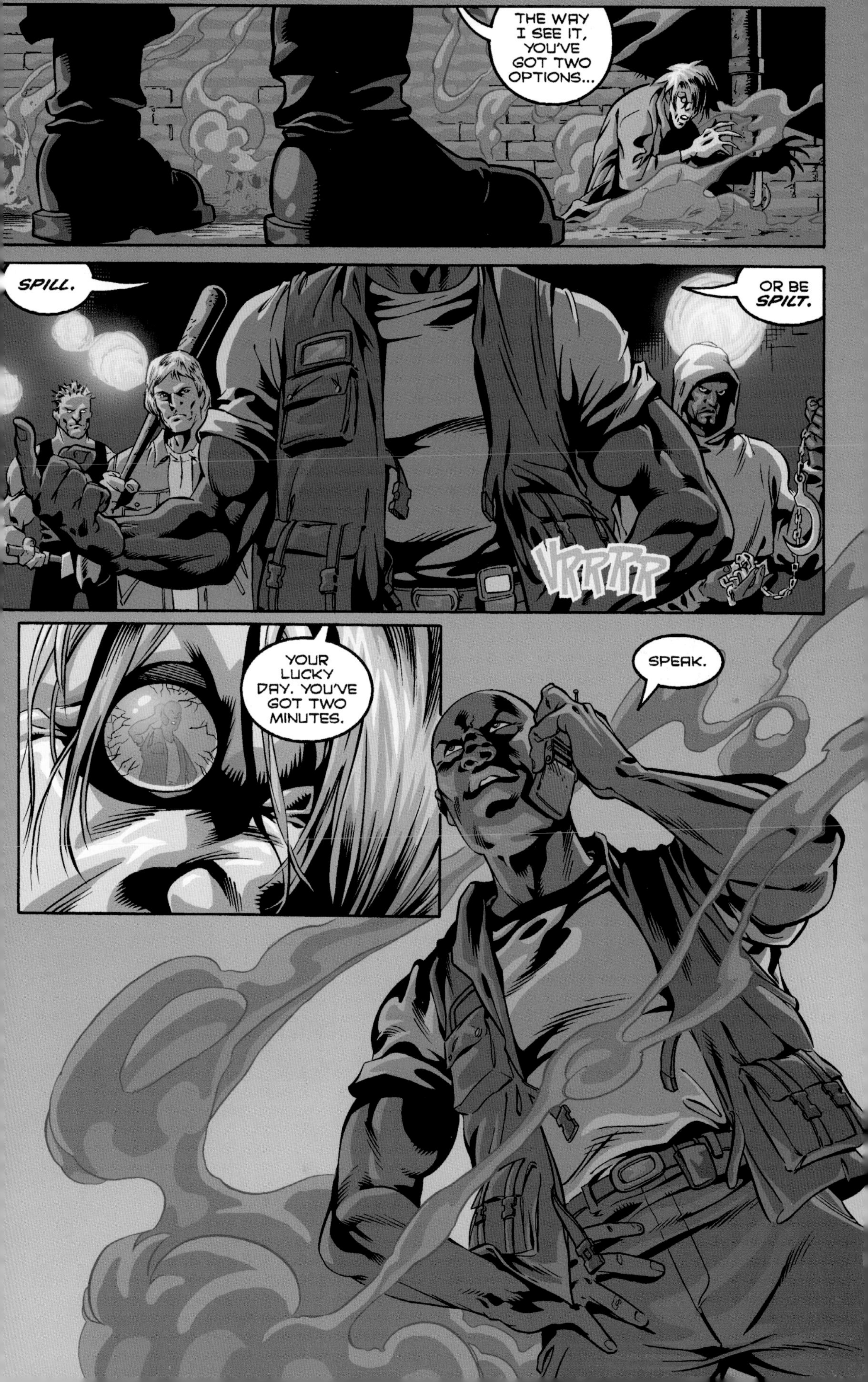
THE WAY I SEE IT, YOU'VE GOT TWO OPTIONS...
SPILL.
OR BE SPILT.
VRRRRR
YOUR LUCKY DAY. YOU'VE GOT TWO MINUTES.
SPEAK.

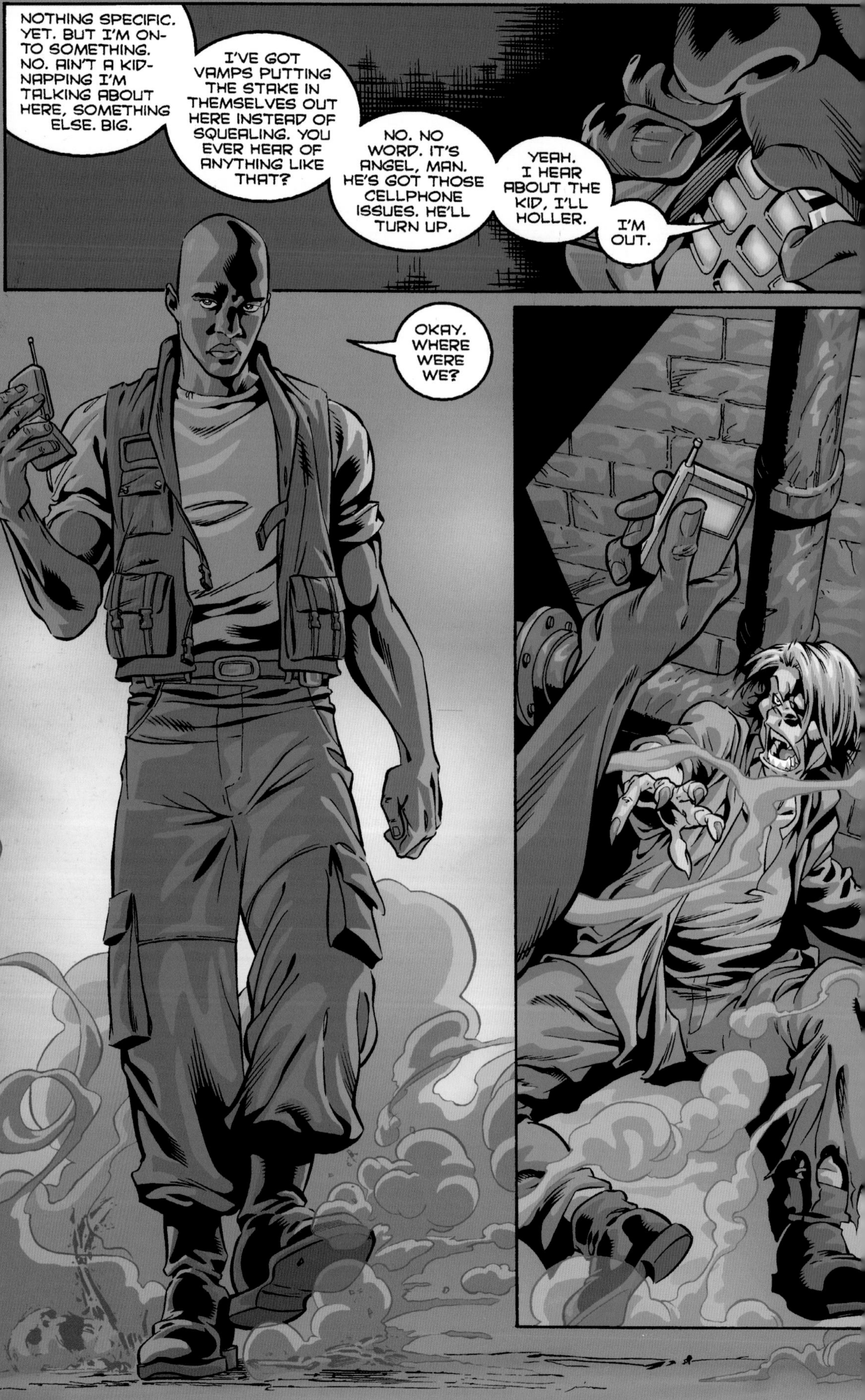
NOTHING SPECIFIC. YET. BUT I'M ON-TO SOMETHING. NO. AIN'T A KID-NAPPING I'M TALKING ABOUT HERE, SOMETHING ELSE. BIG.
I'VE GOT VAMPS PUTTING THE STAKE IN THEMSELVES OUT HERE INSTEAD OF SQUEALING. YOU EVER HEAR OF ANYTHING LIKE THAT?
NO. NO WORD. IT'S ANGEL, MAN. HE'S GOT THOSE CELLPHONE ISSUES. HE'LL TURN UP.
YEAH. I HEAR ABOUT THE KID, I'LL HOLLER.
I'M OUT.
OKAY. WHERE WERE WE?

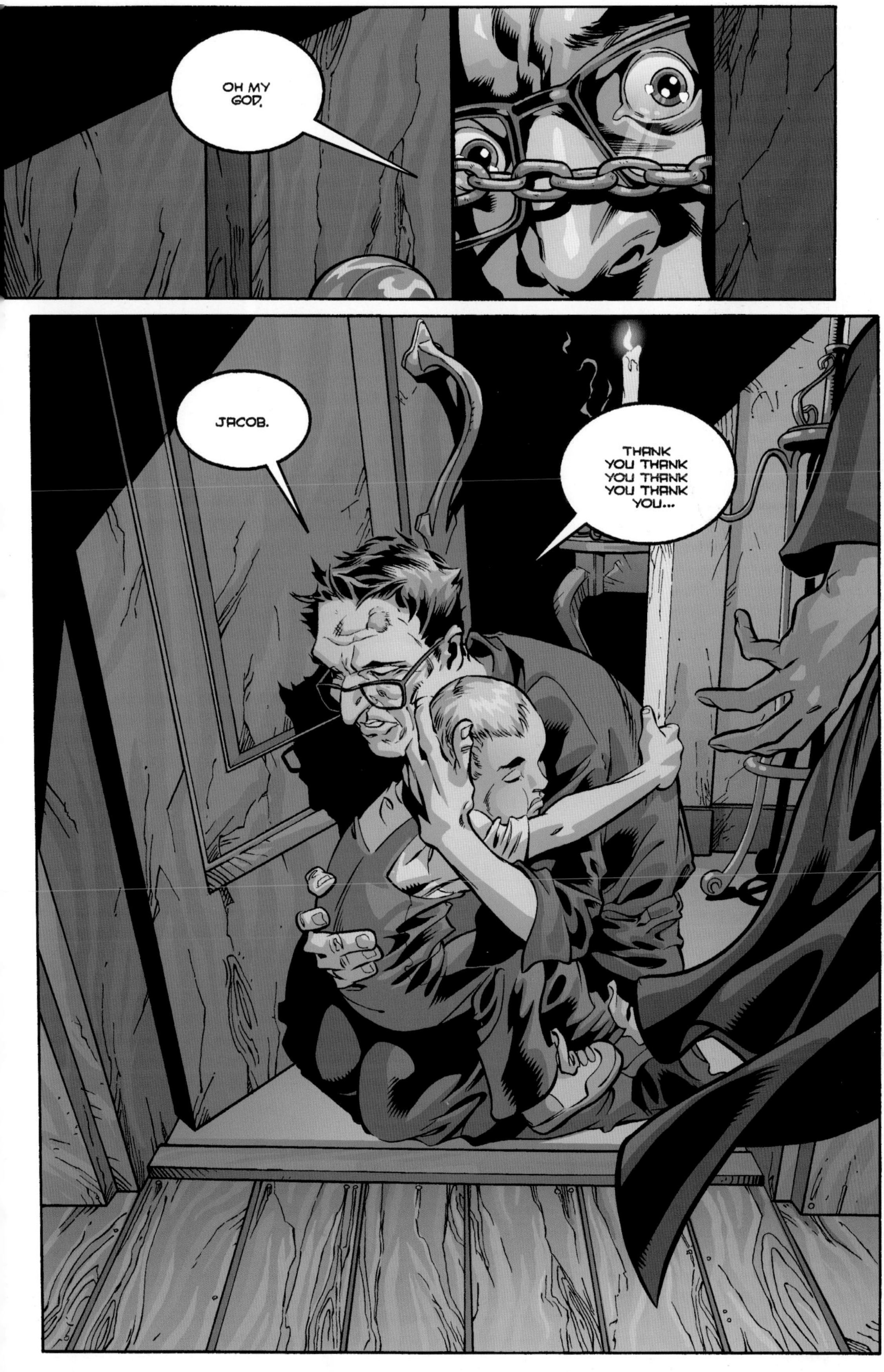
OH MY GOD.
JACOB.
THANK YOU THANK YOU THANK YOU THANK YOU...

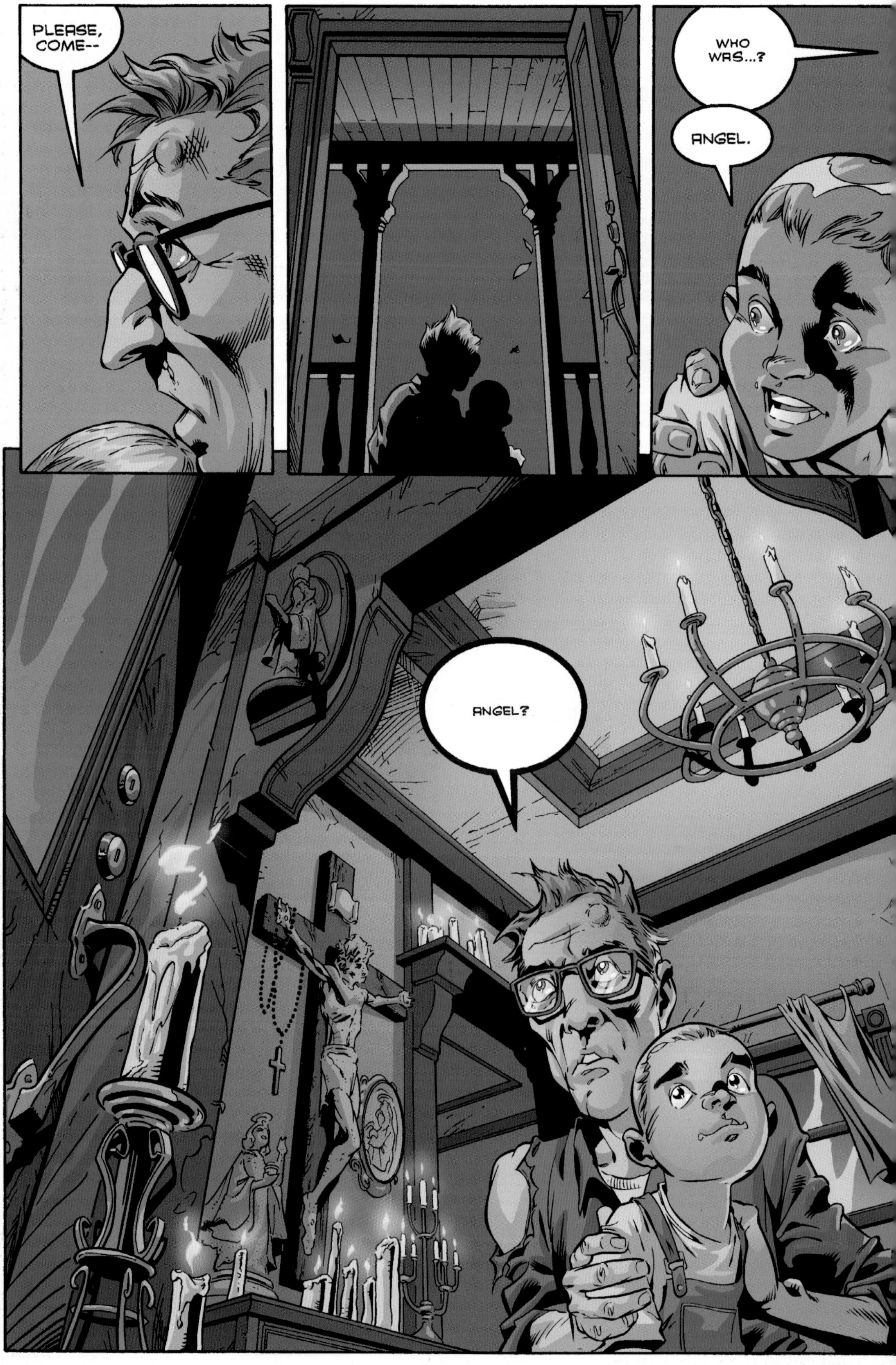
PLEASE, COME--
WHO WAS...?
ANGEL.
ANGEL?

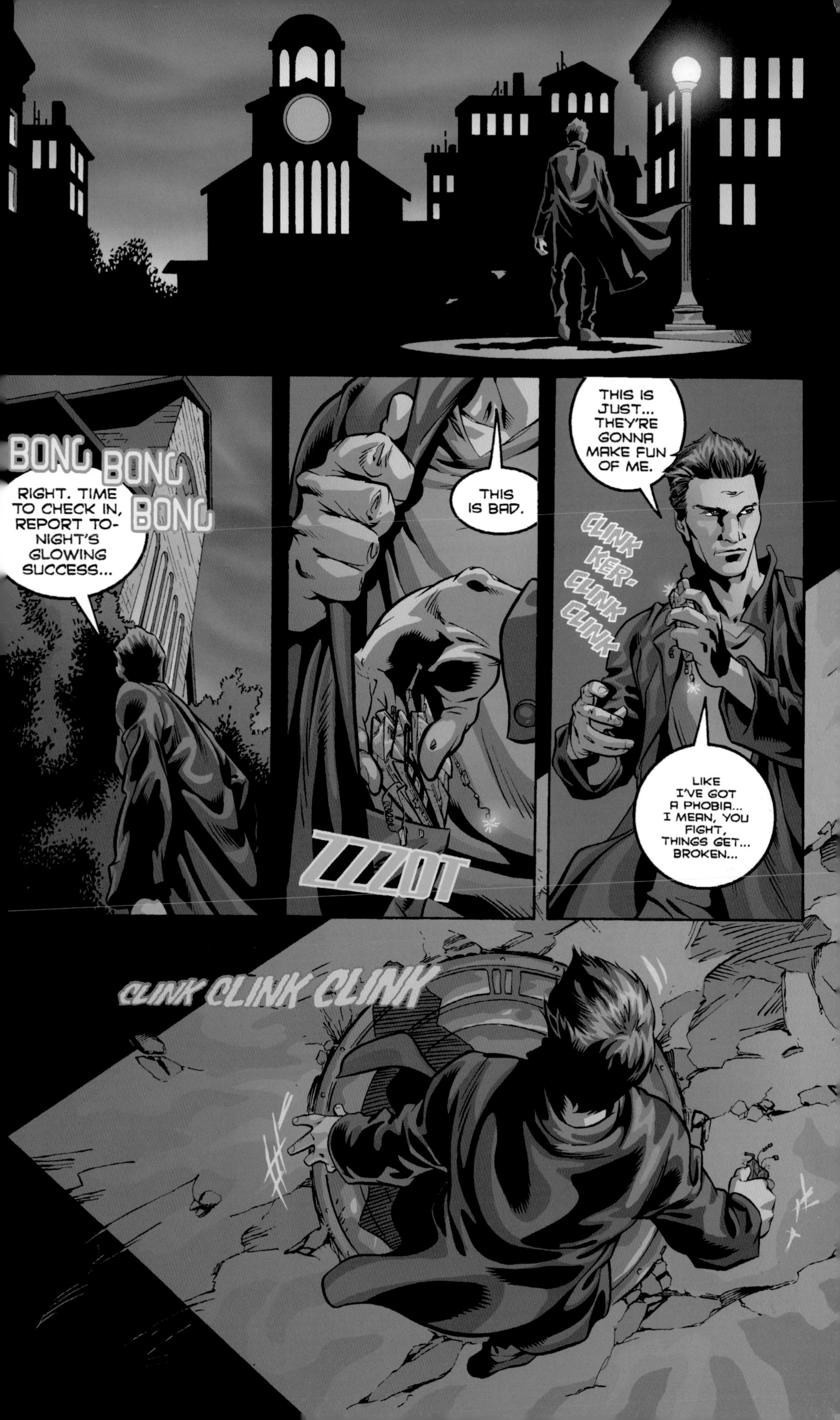
BONG BONG BONG
RIGHT. TIME TO CHECK IN, REPORT TO-NIGHT'S GLOWING SUCCESS...
THIS IS BAD.
ZZZOT
THIS IS JUST... THEY'RE GONNA MAKE FUN OF ME.
CLINK KER-CLINK CLINK CLINK
LIKE I'VE GOT A PHOBIA... I MEAN, YOU FIGHT, THINGS GET... BROKEN...
CLINK CLINK CLINK

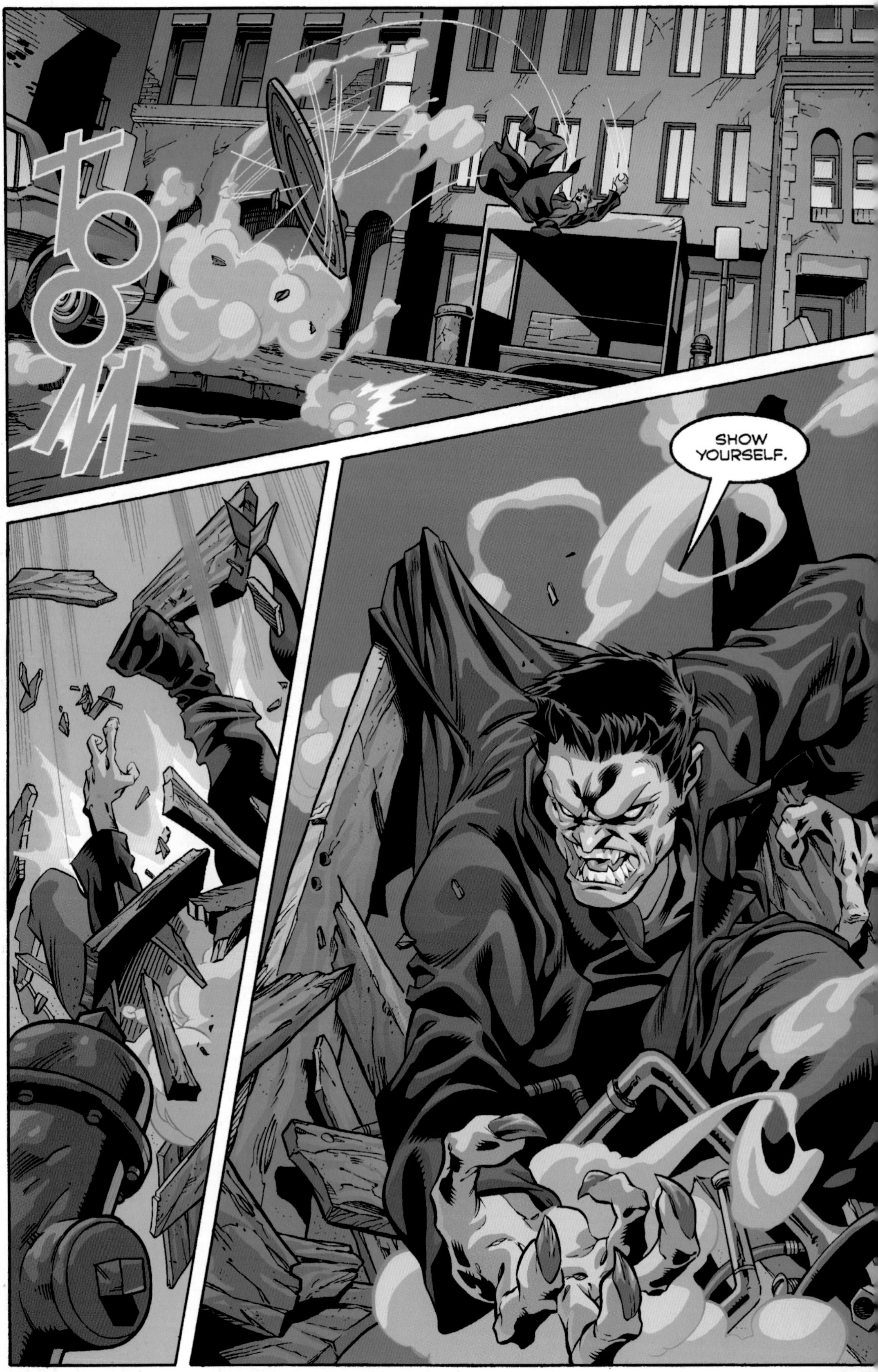
tooM
SHOW YOURSELF.

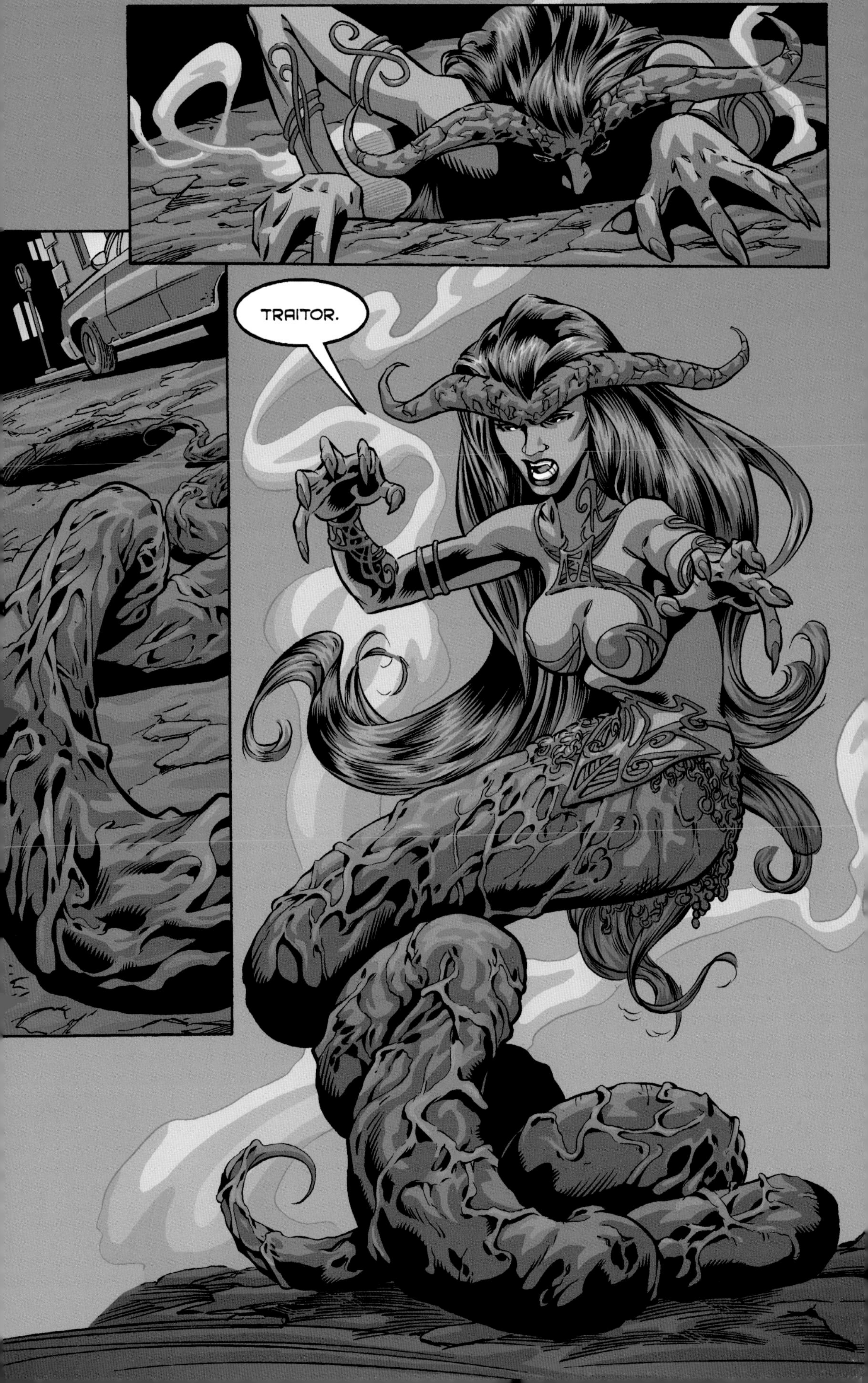
TRAITOR.

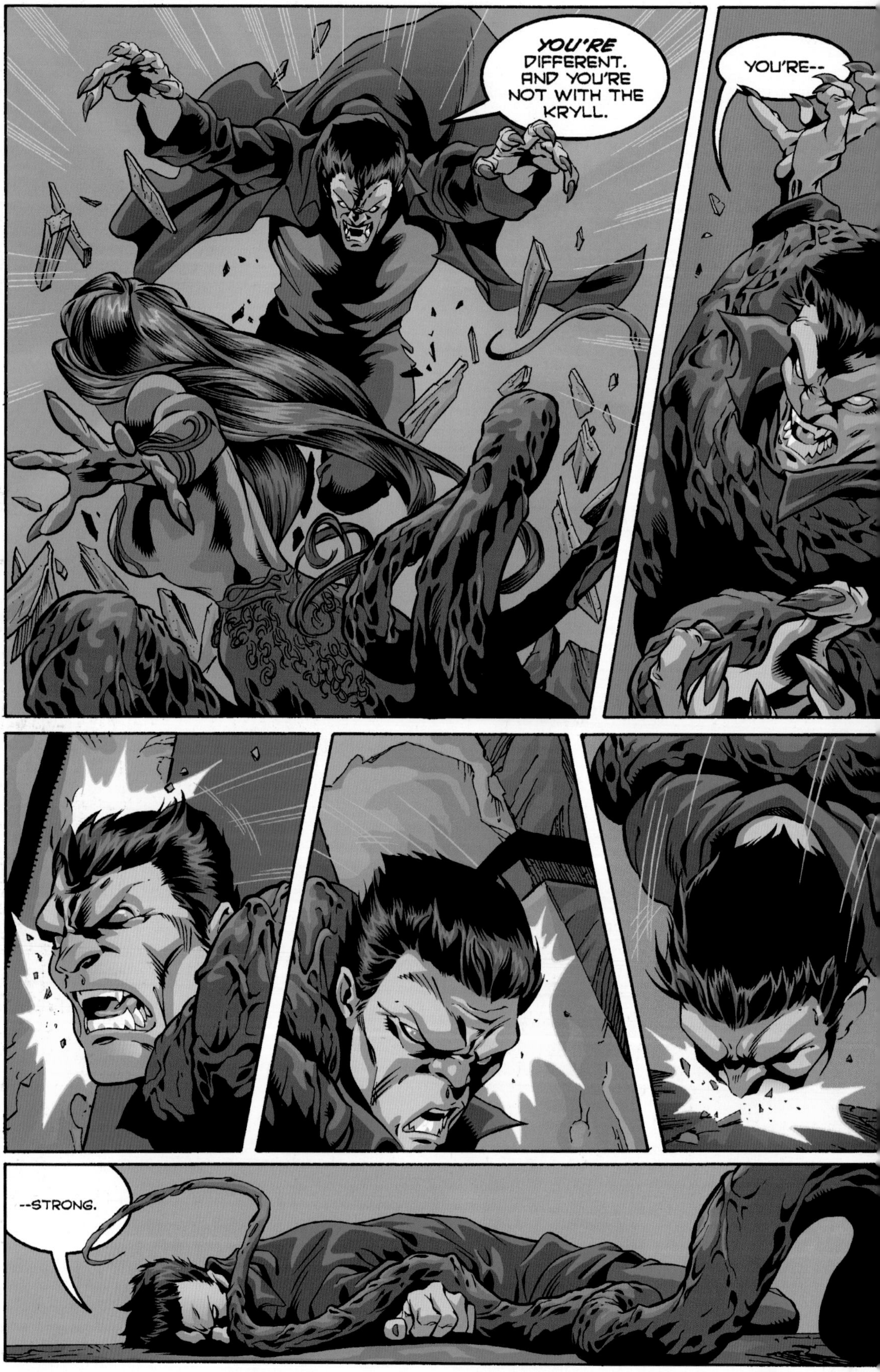

YOU'RE DIFFERENT. AND YOU'RE NOT WITH THE KRYLL.
YOU'RE--
--STRONG.

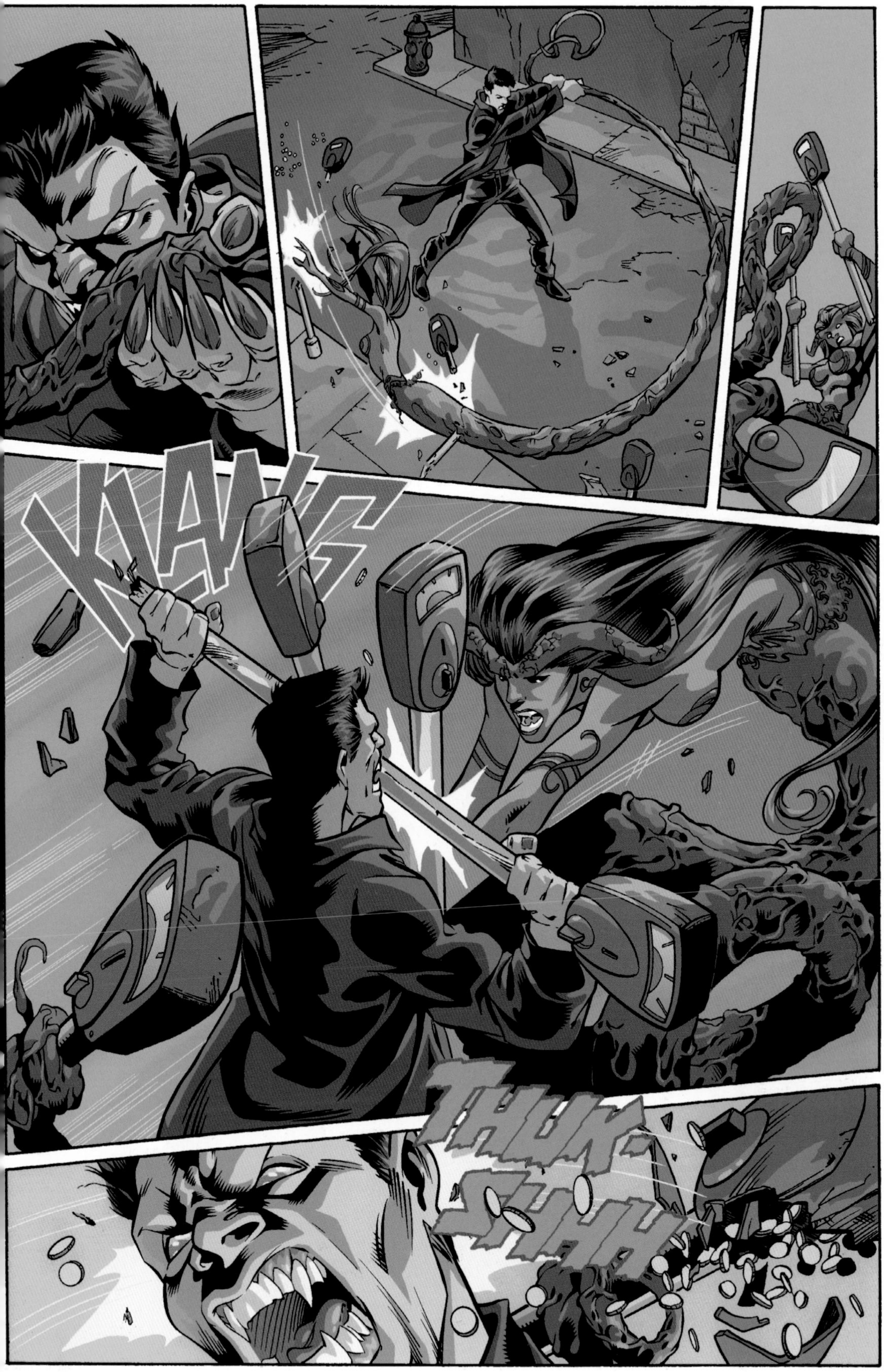
KLANG
THUK-SHHH

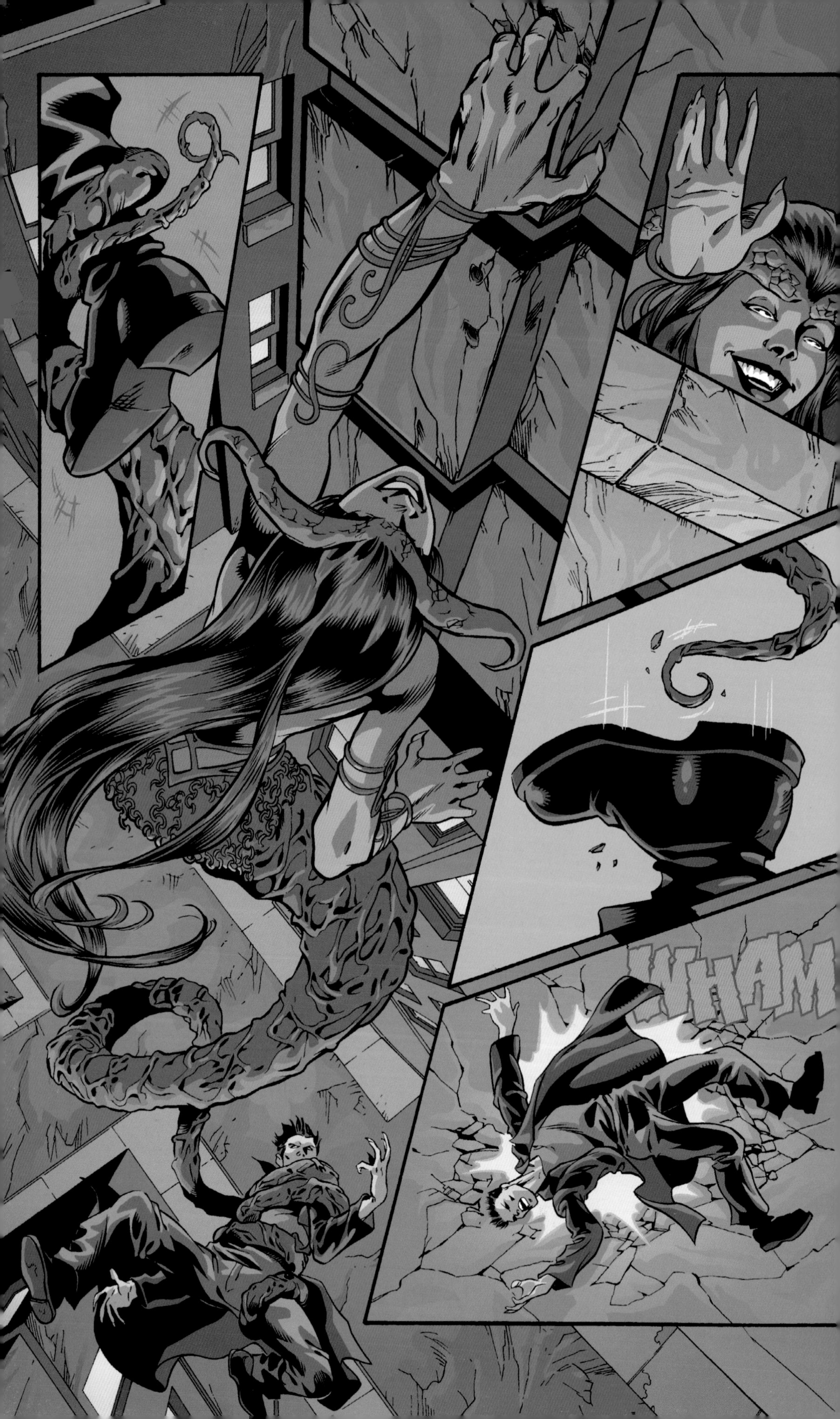
WHAM

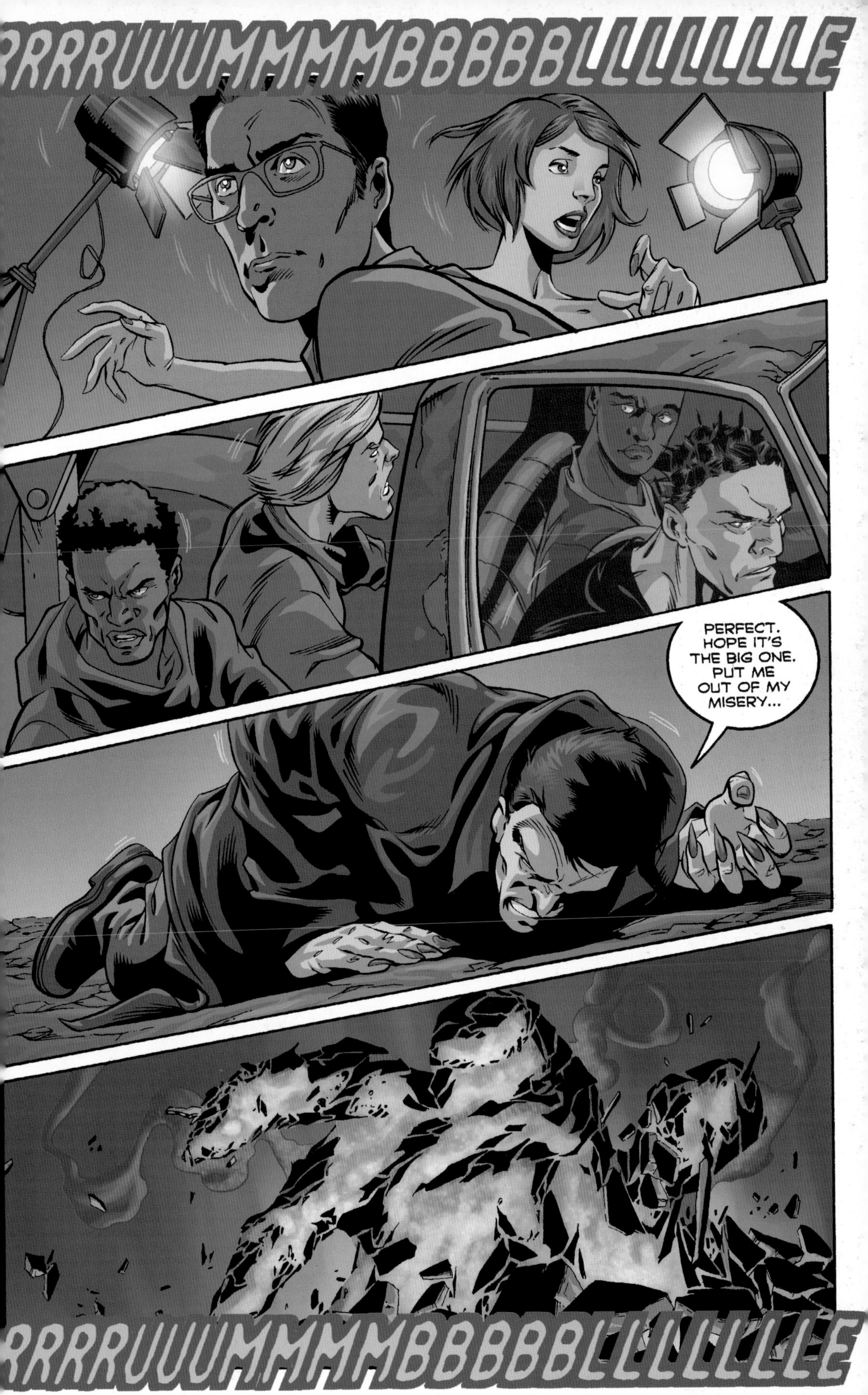
RRRRUUUMMMMBBBBBLLLLLLLLE
PERFECT. HOPE IT'S THE BIG ONE. PUT ME OUT OF MY MISERY...
RRRRUUUMMMMBBBBBLLLLLLLLE

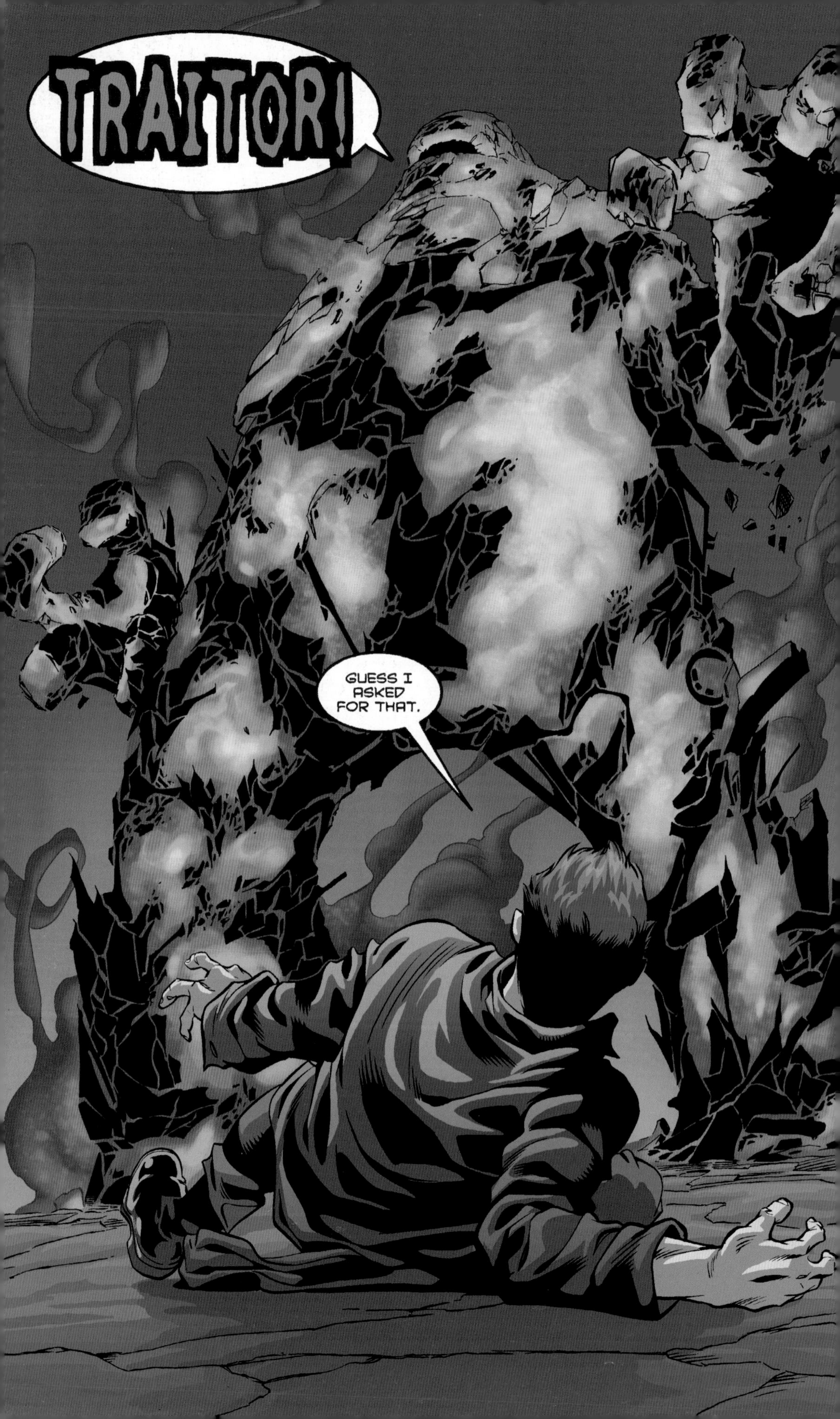
TRAITOR!
GUESS I ASKED FOR THAT.

Two

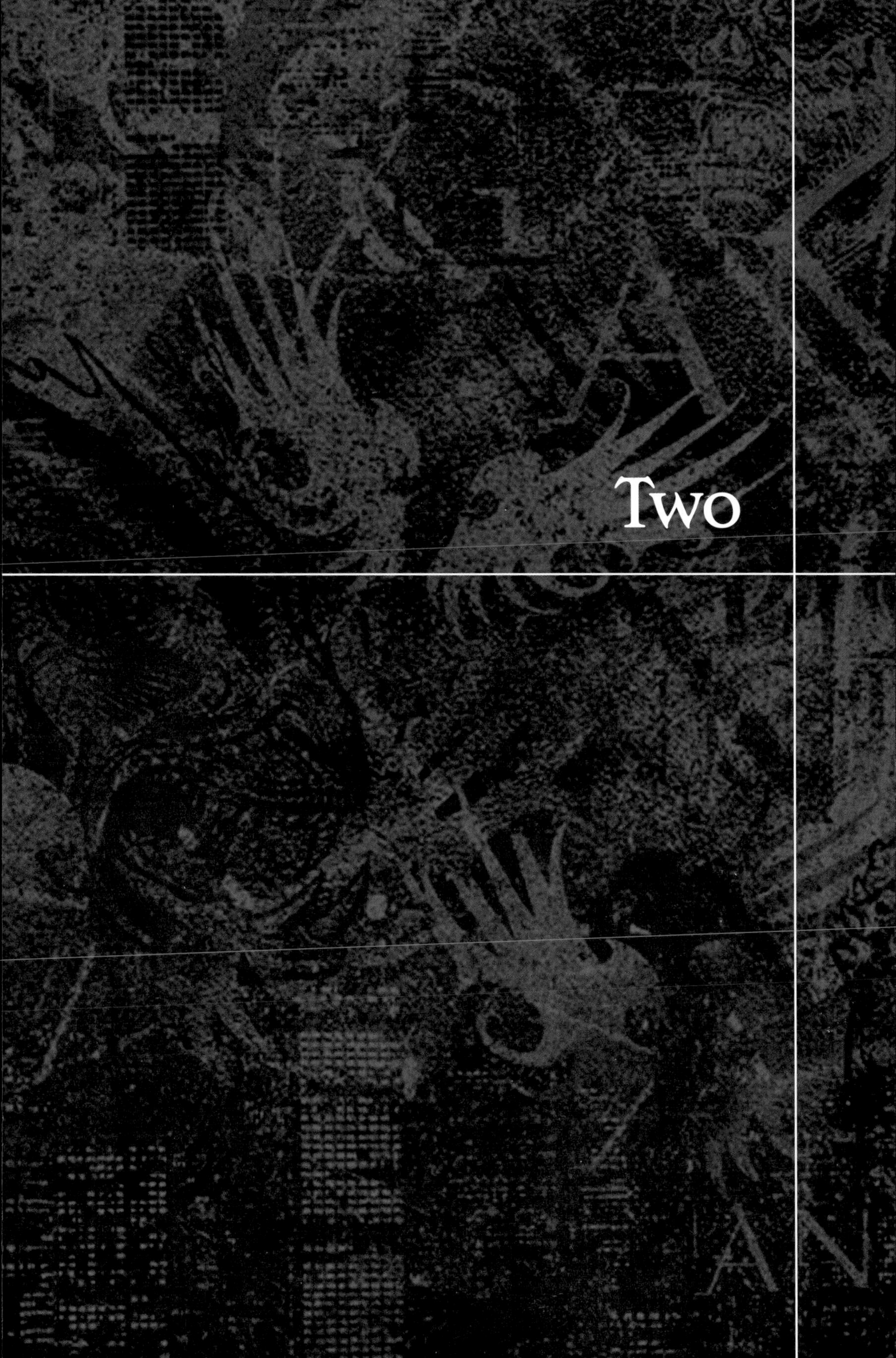

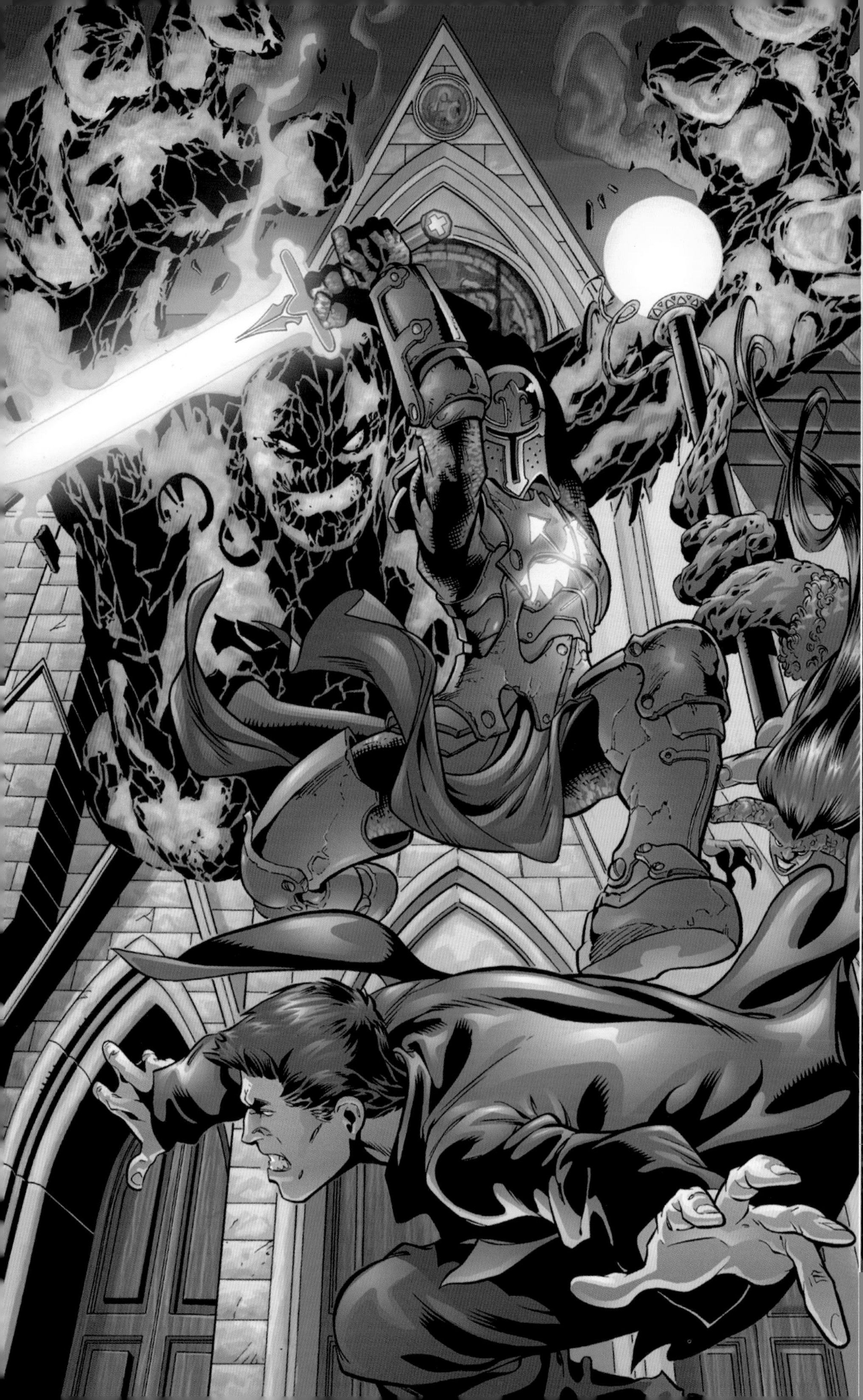

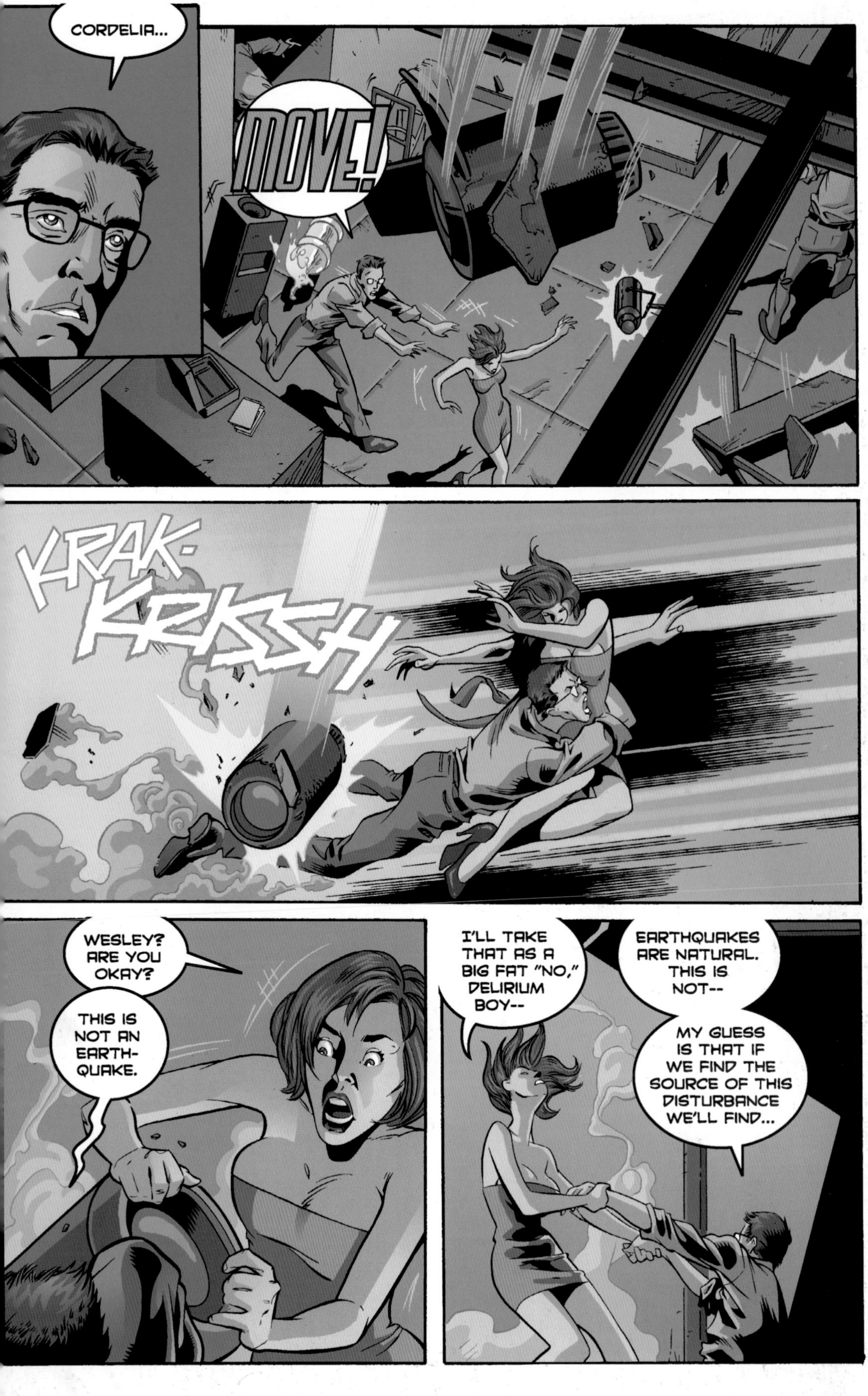
CORDELIA...
MOVE!
KRAK-KRKSH
WESLEY? ARE YOU OKAY?
THIS IS NOT AN EARTH-QUAKE.
I'LL TAKE THAT AS A BIG FAT "NO," DELIRIUM BOY--
EARTHQUAKES ARE NATURAL. THIS IS NOT--
MY GUESS IS THAT IF WE FIND THE SOURCE OF THIS DISTURBANCE WE'LL FIND...

"...ANGEL."
LOS ANGELES.
OVER THREE HUNDRED DAYS OF SUNSHINE A YEAR, ON AVERAGE.
SO WHY COULDN'T IT BE A CONVERTIBLE?
LONG NIGHT'S JOURNEY PART 2:
ROCK AND A HARD PLACE

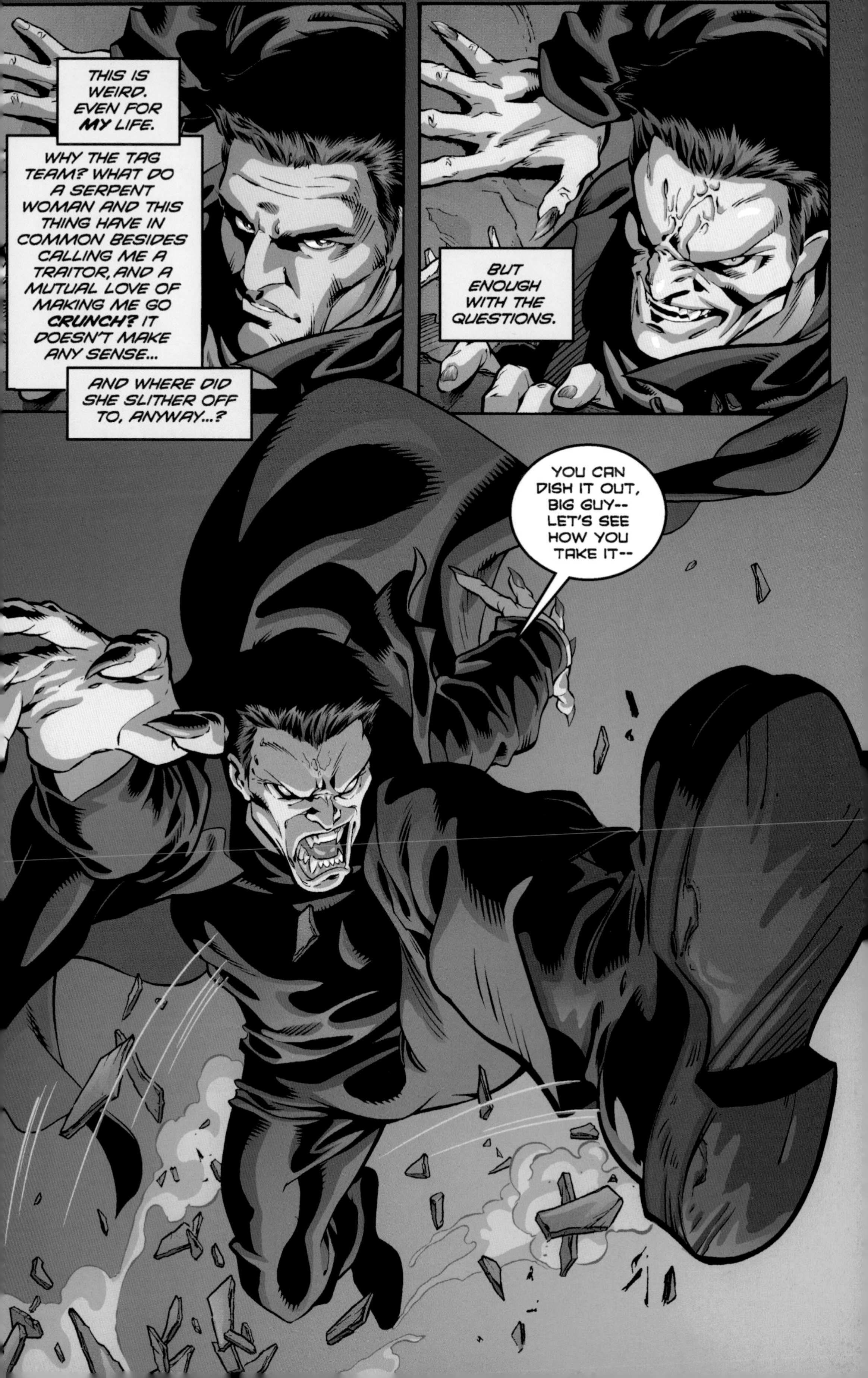
THIS IS WEIRD. EVEN FOR **MY** LIFE.
WHY THE TAG TEAM? WHAT DO A SERPENT WOMAN AND THIS THING HAVE IN COMMON BESIDES CALLING ME A TRAITOR, AND A MUTUAL LOVE OF MAKING ME GO **CRUNCH?** IT DOESN'T MAKE ANY SENSE...
AND WHERE DID SHE SLITHER OFF TO, ANYWAY...?
BUT ENOUGH WITH THE QUESTIONS.
YOU CAN DISH IT OUT, BIG GUY-- LET'S SEE HOW YOU TAKE IT--

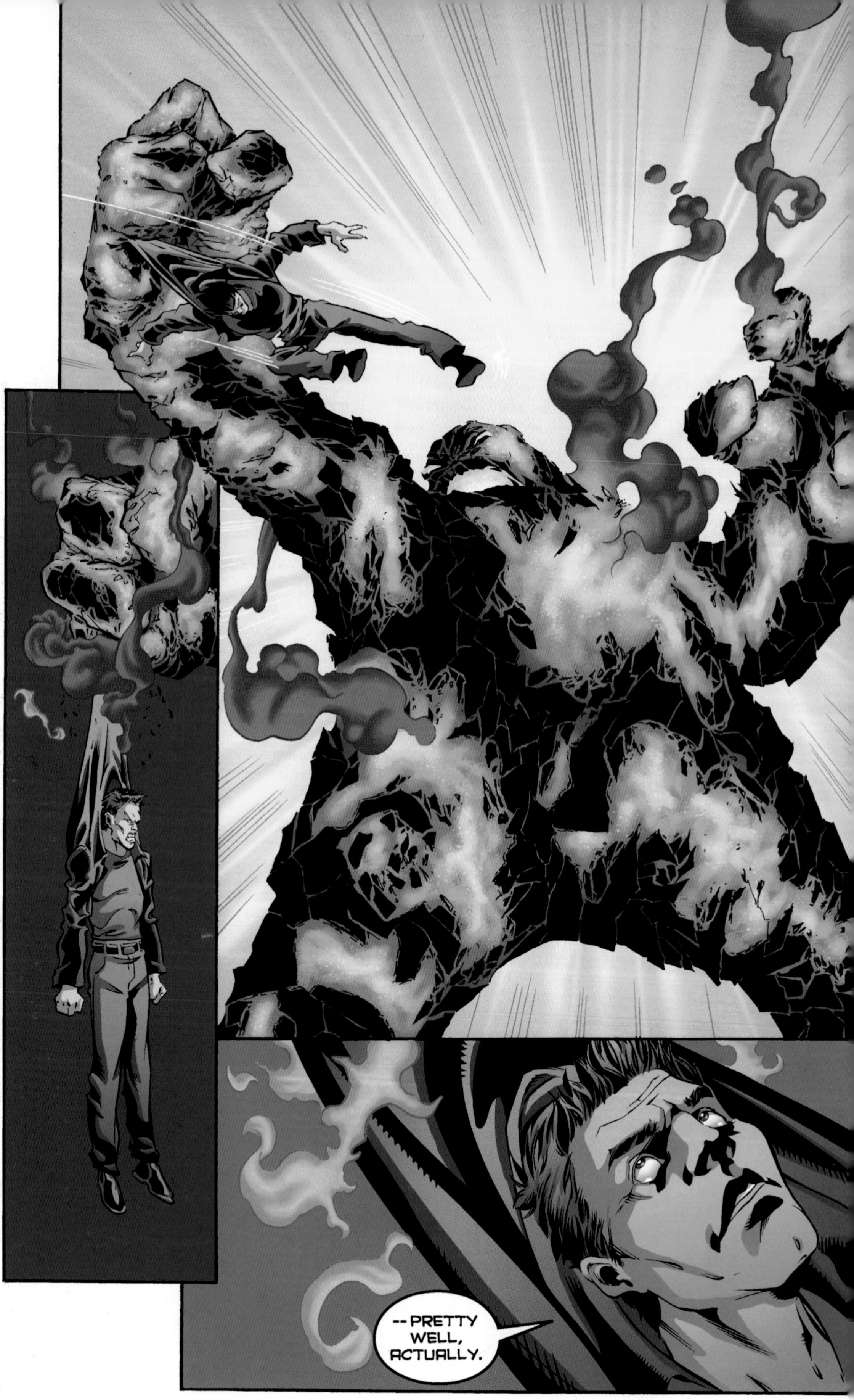
--PRETTY WELL, ACTUALLY.

SLUK
GLUK
GLUK

KWOOSH

NO OFFENSE, BUT I'M NOT GOOD WITH THIS KIND OF HEAT. IRISH AND ALL.

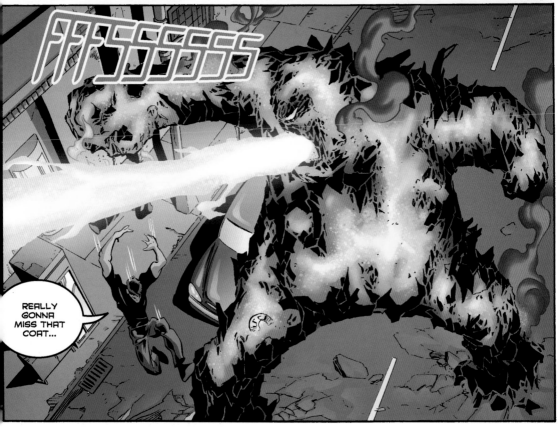

FFFSSSSSS

REALLY GONNA MISS THAT COAT...

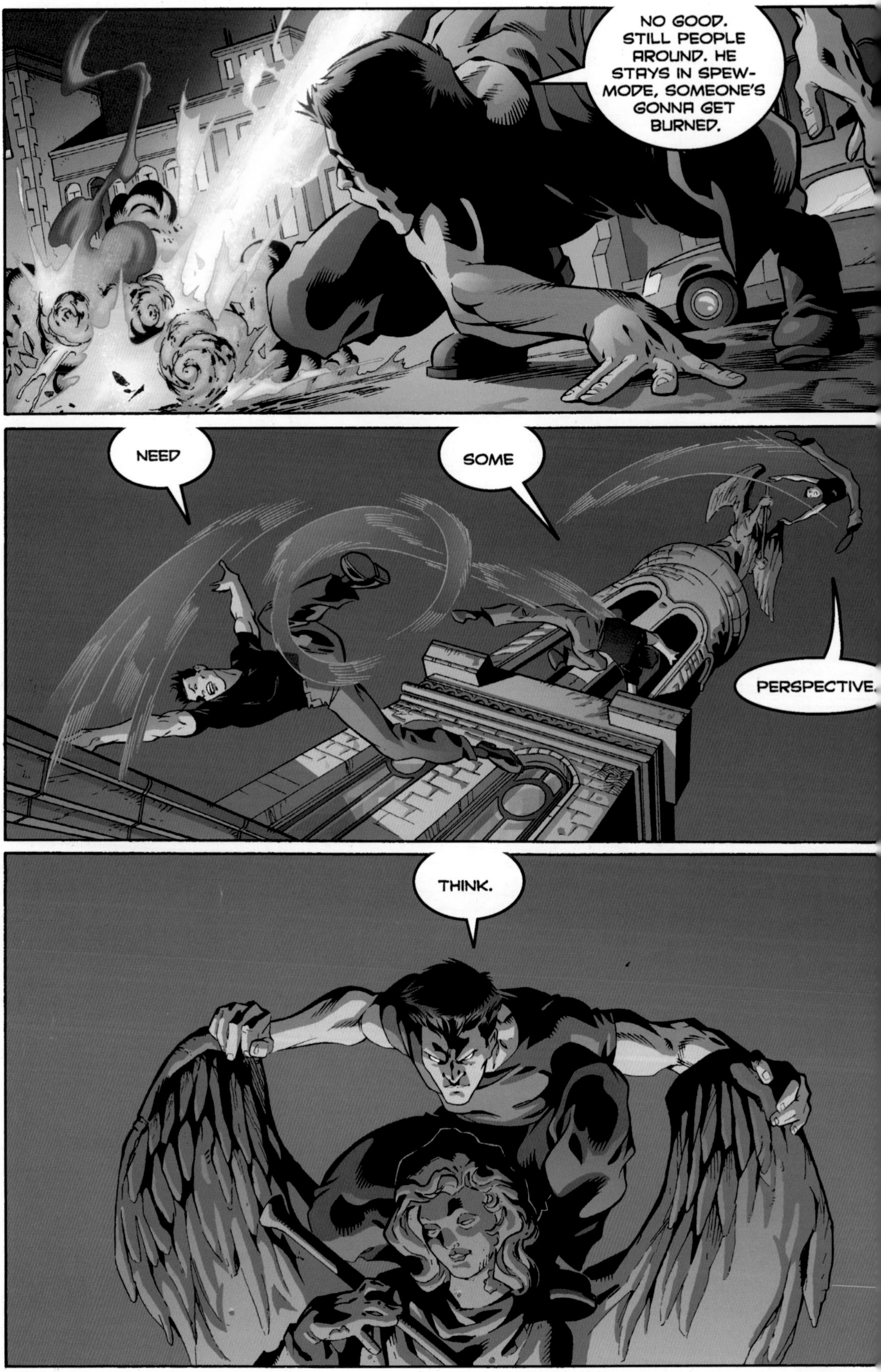
NO GOOD. STILL PEOPLE AROUND. HE STAYS IN SPEW-MODE, SOMEONE'S GONNA GET BURNED.
NEED
SOME
PERSPECTIVE.
THINK.

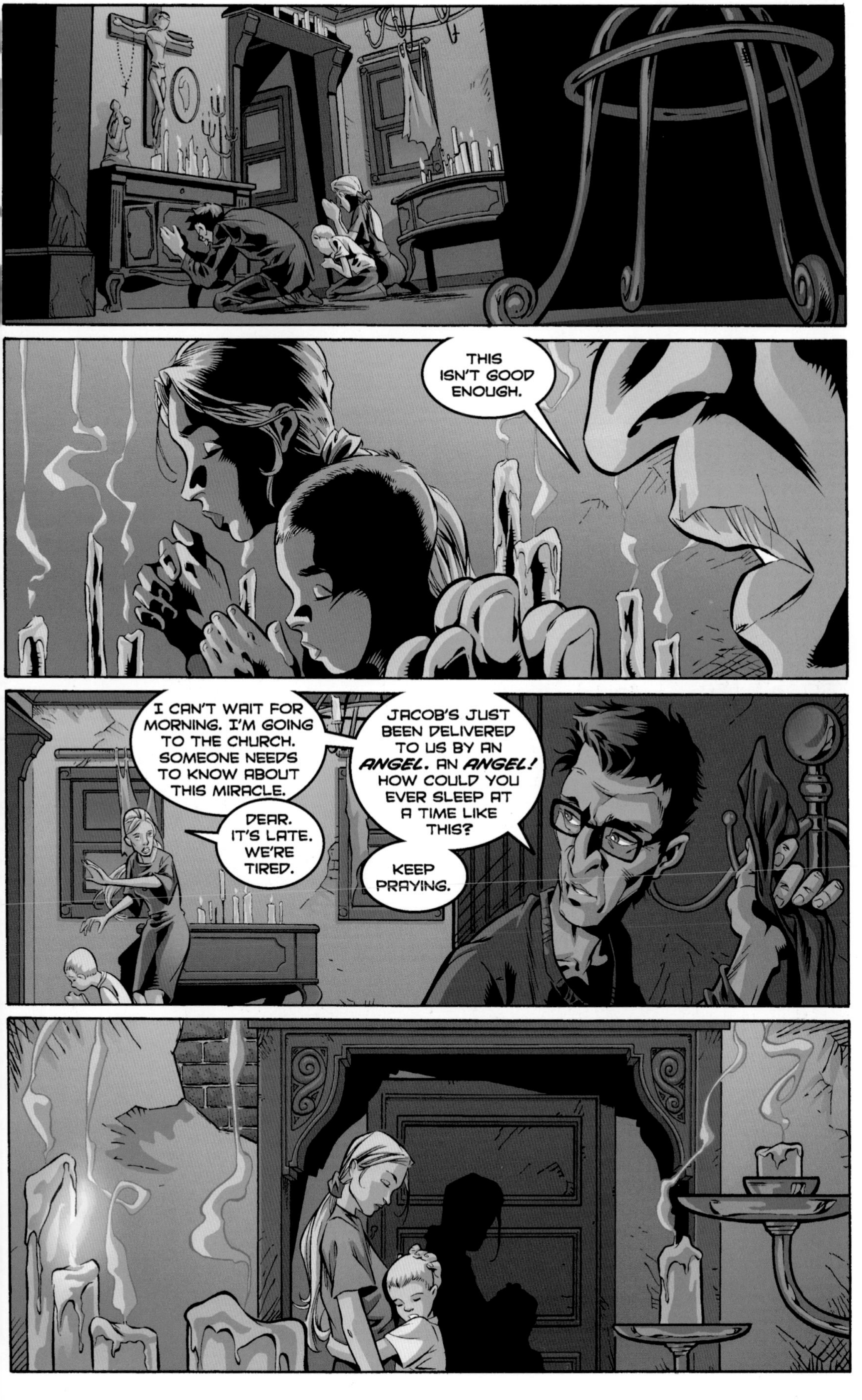
THIS ISN'T GOOD ENOUGH.
I CAN'T WAIT FOR MORNING. I'M GOING TO THE CHURCH. SOMEONE NEEDS TO KNOW ABOUT THIS MIRACLE.
DEAR. IT'S LATE. WE'RE TIRED.
JACOB'S JUST BEEN DELIVERED TO US BY AN ANGEL. AN ANGEL! HOW COULD YOU EVER SLEEP AT A TIME LIKE THIS?
KEEP PRAYING.

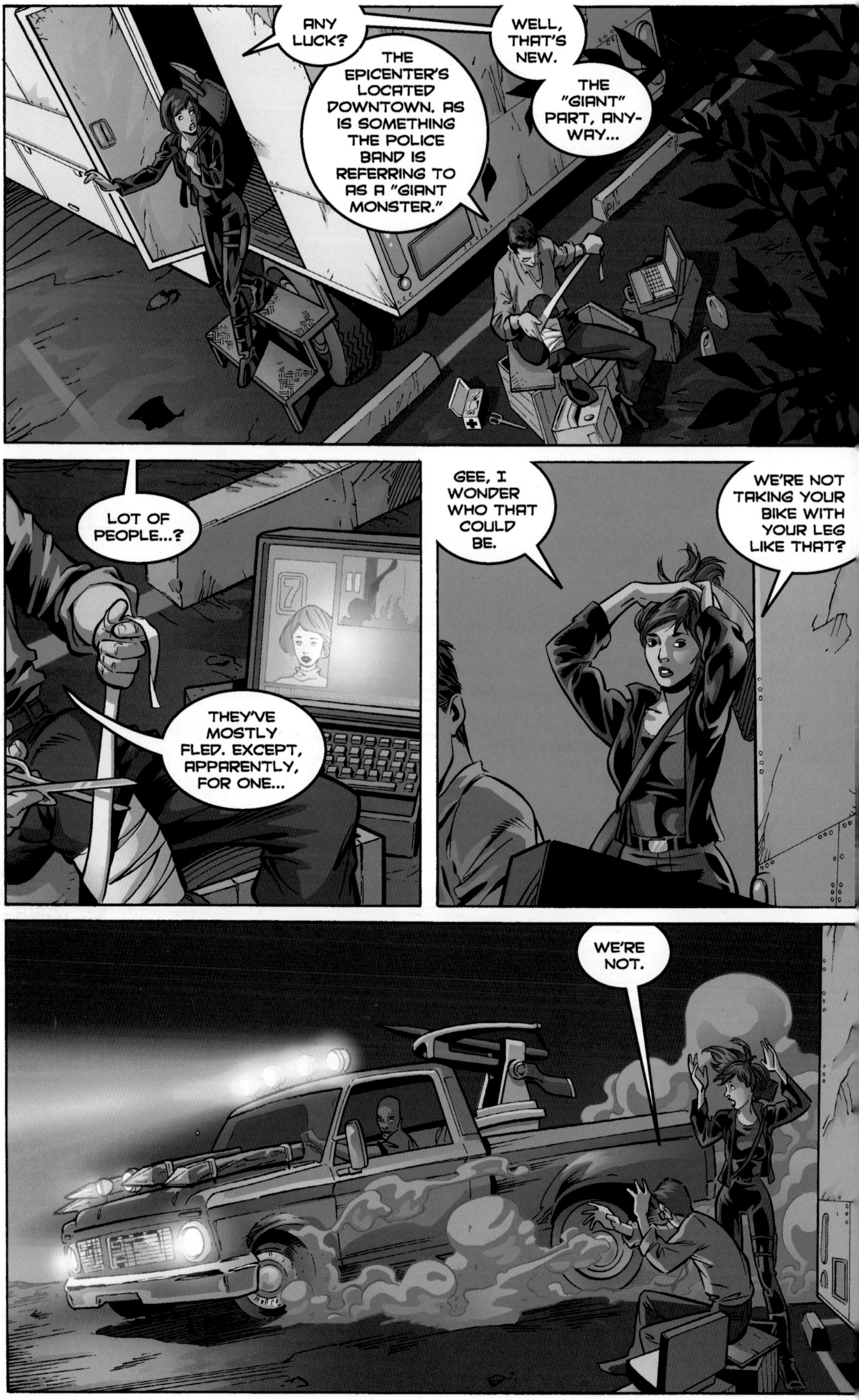
ANY LUCK?
THE EPICENTER'S LOCATED DOWNTOWN. AS IS SOMETHING THE POLICE BAND IS REFERRING TO AS A "GIANT MONSTER."
WELL, THAT'S NEW.
THE "GIANT" PART, ANY-WAY...
LOT OF PEOPLE...?
THEY'VE MOSTLY FLED. EXCEPT, APPARENTLY, FOR ONE...
GEE, I WONDER WHO THAT COULD BE.
WE'RE NOT TAKING YOUR BIKE WITH YOUR LEG LIKE THAT?
WE'RE NOT.

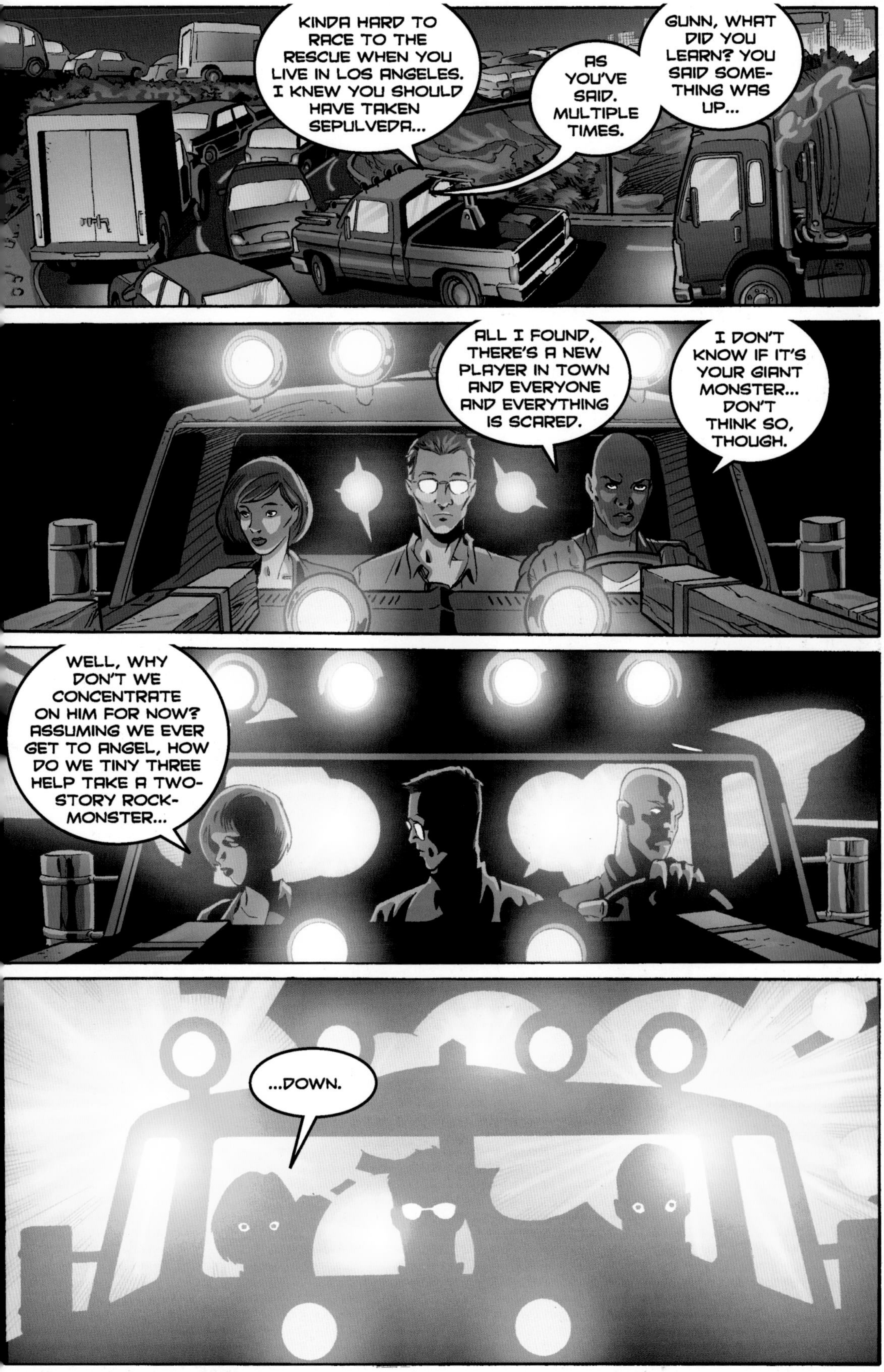
KINDA HARD TO RACE TO THE RESCUE WHEN YOU LIVE IN LOS ANGELES. I KNEW YOU SHOULD HAVE TAKEN SEPULVEDA...
AS YOU'VE SAID. MULTIPLE TIMES.
GUNN, WHAT DID YOU LEARN? YOU SAID SOME-THING WAS UP...
ALL I FOUND, THERE'S A NEW PLAYER IN TOWN AND EVERYONE AND EVERYTHING IS SCARED.
I DON'T KNOW IF IT'S YOUR GIANT MONSTER... DON'T THINK SO, THOUGH.
WELL, WHY DON'T WE CONCENTRATE ON HIM FOR NOW? ASSUMING WE EVER GET TO ANGEL, HOW DO WE TINY THREE HELP TAKE A TWO-STORY ROCK-MONSTER...
...DOWN.

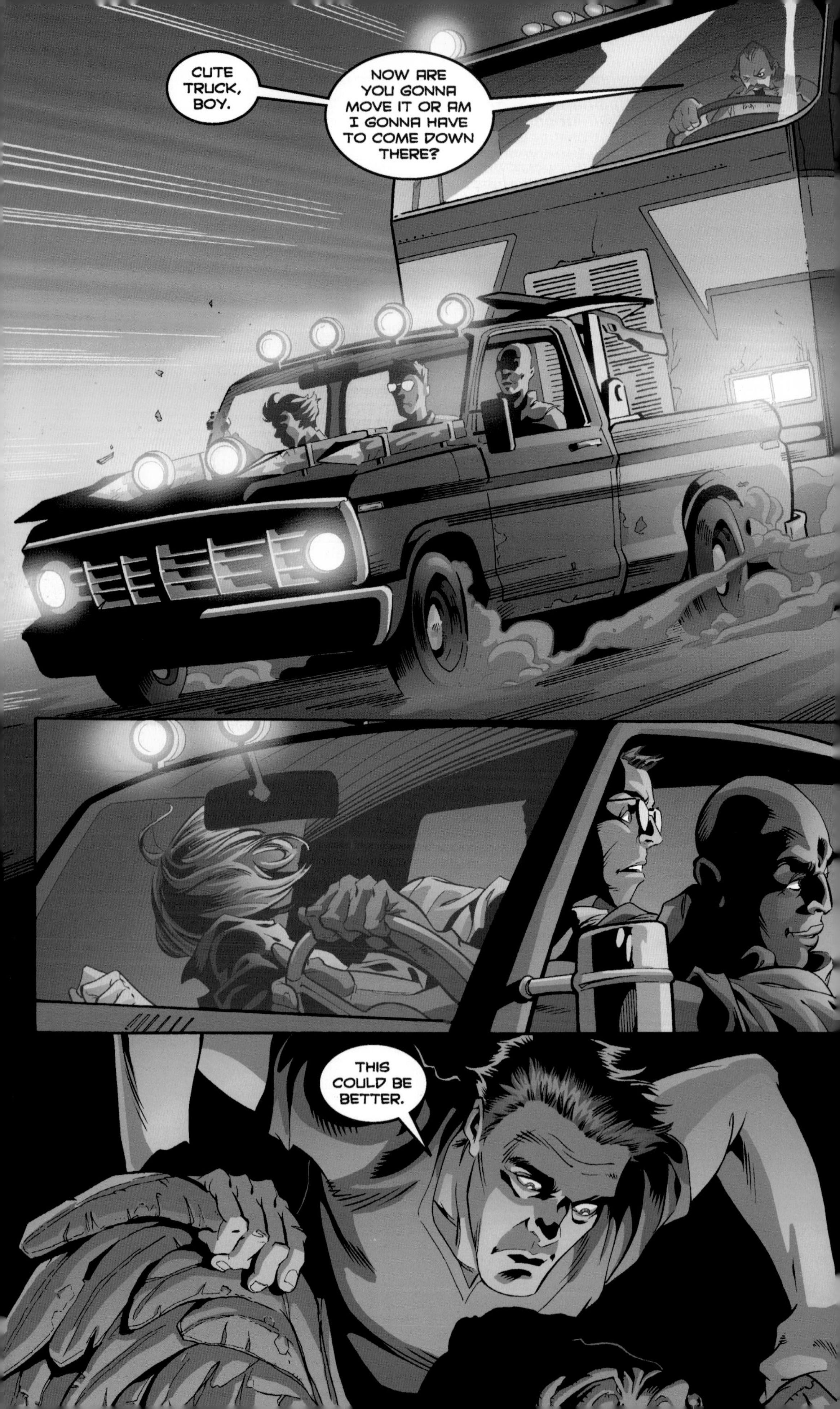
CUTE TRUCK, BOY.
NOW ARE YOU GONNA MOVE IT OR AM I GONNA HAVE TO COME DOWN THERE?
THIS COULD BE BETTER.

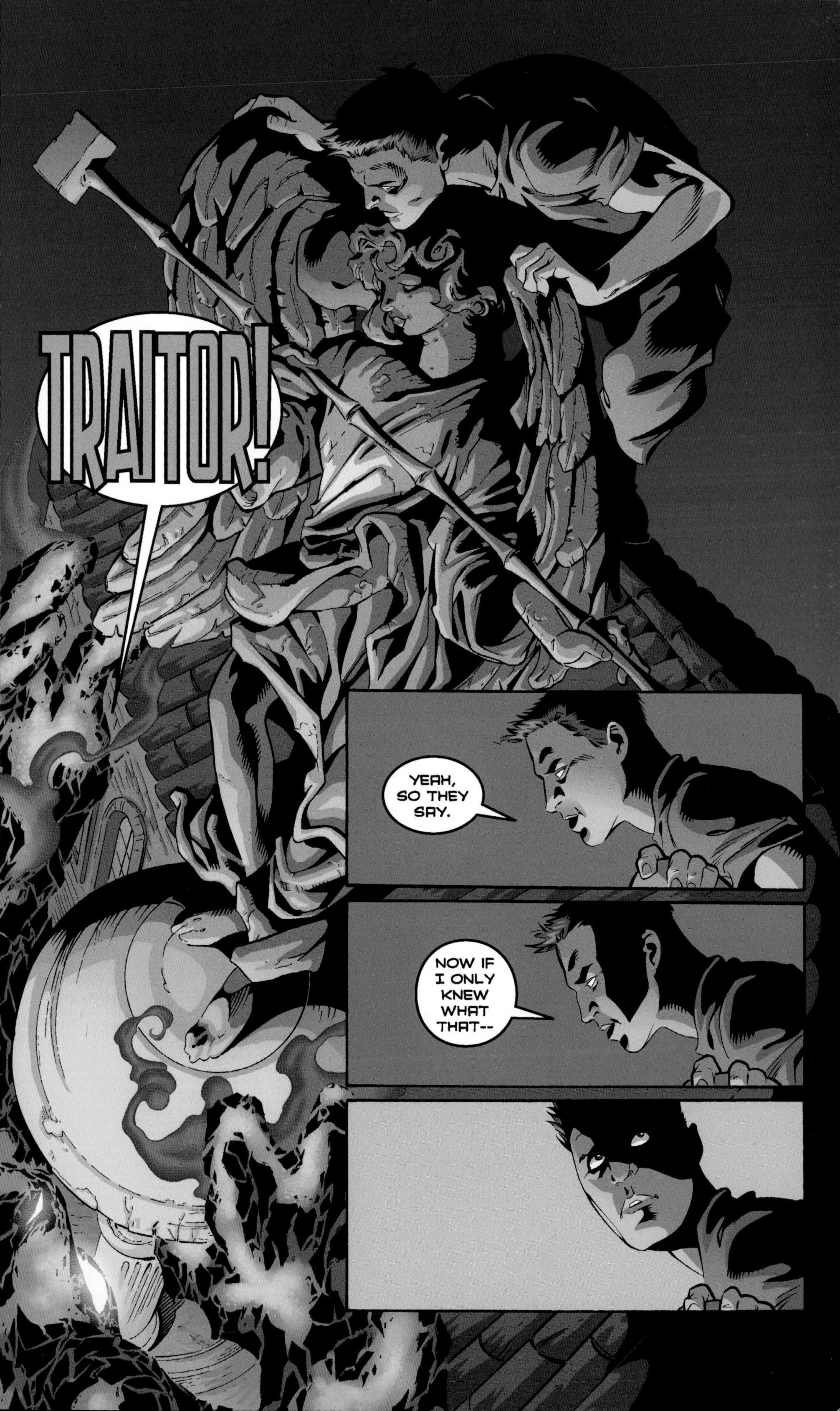
TRAITOR!
YEAH, SO THEY SAY.
NOW IF I ONLY KNEW WHAT THAT--

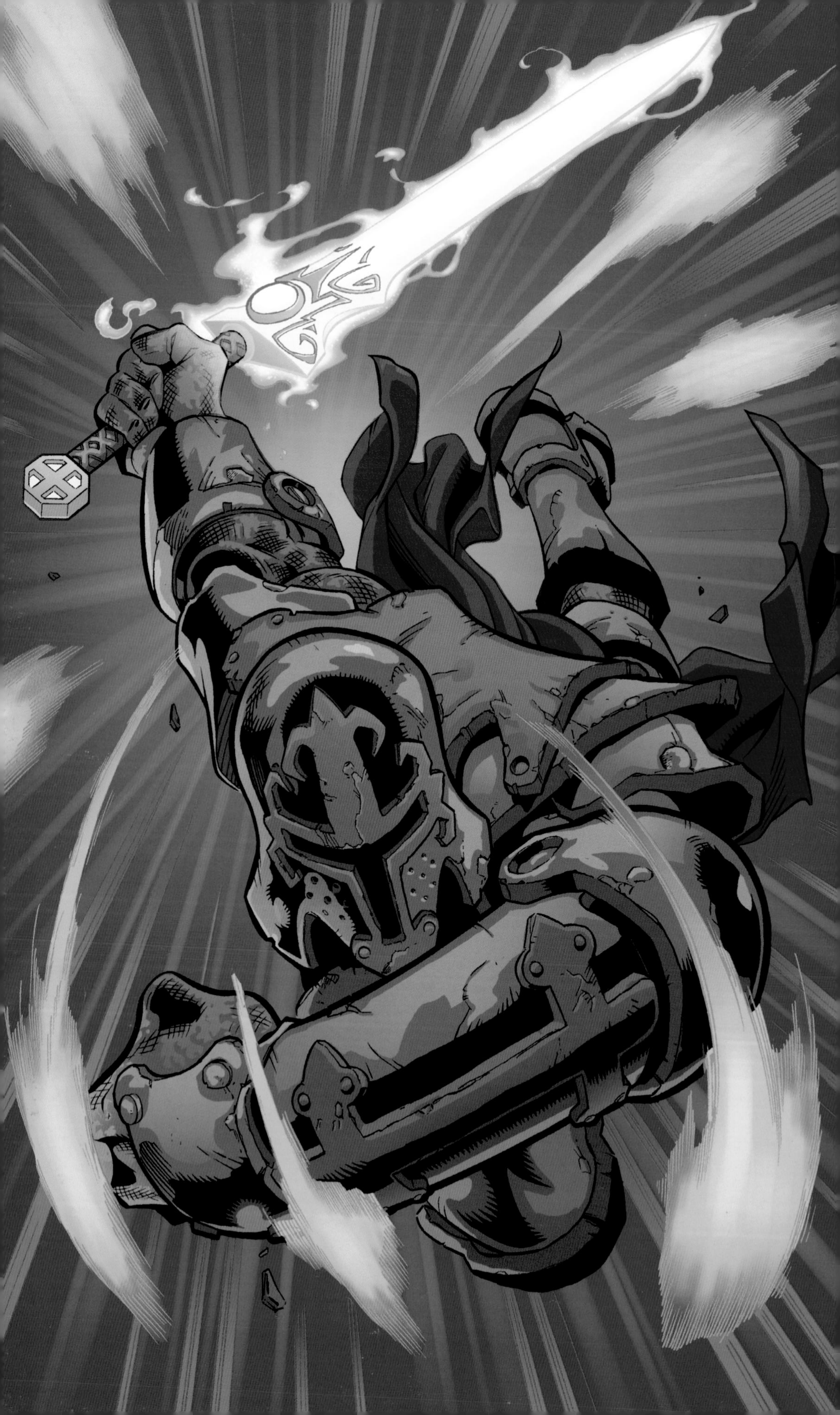

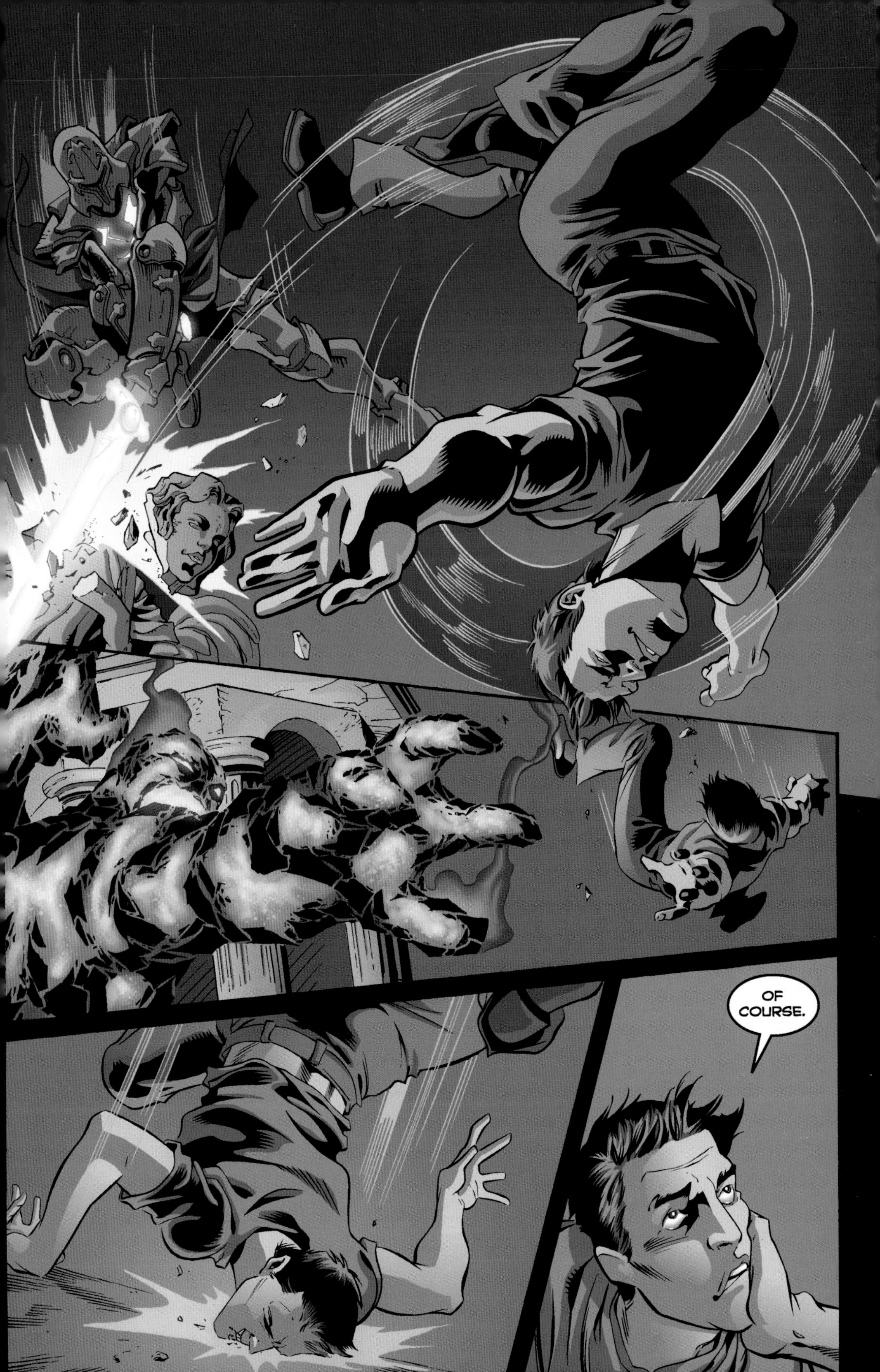
OF COURSE.

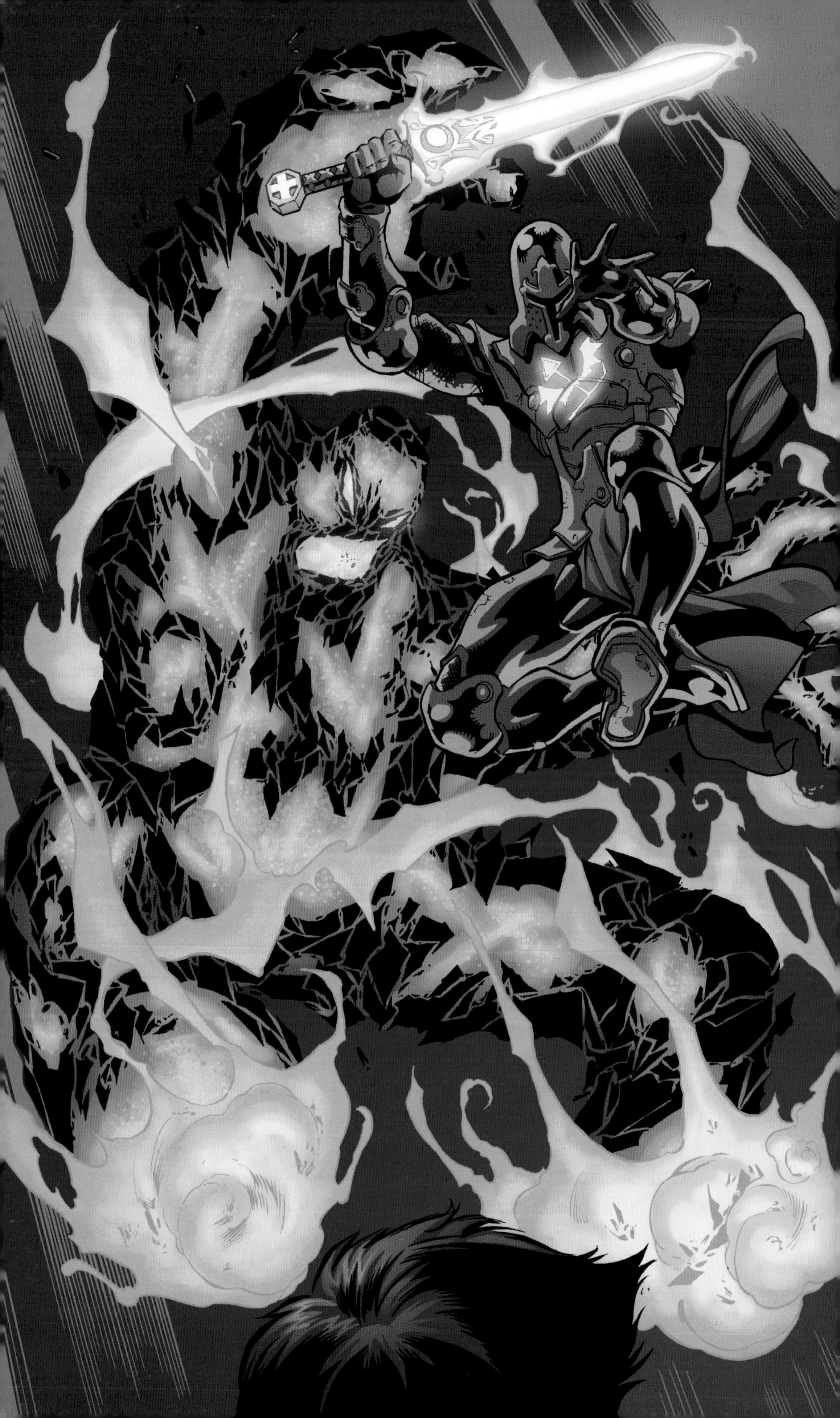

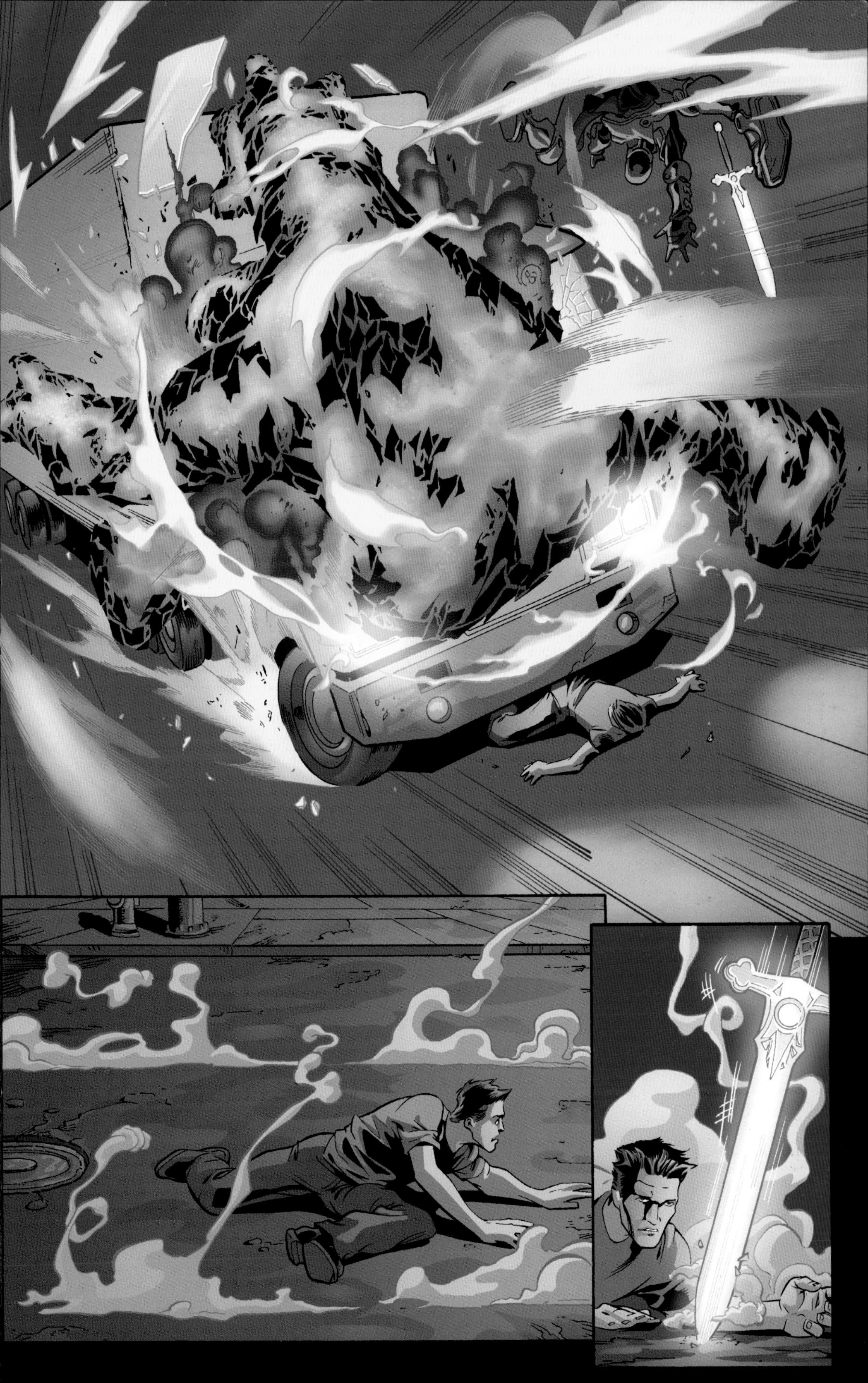

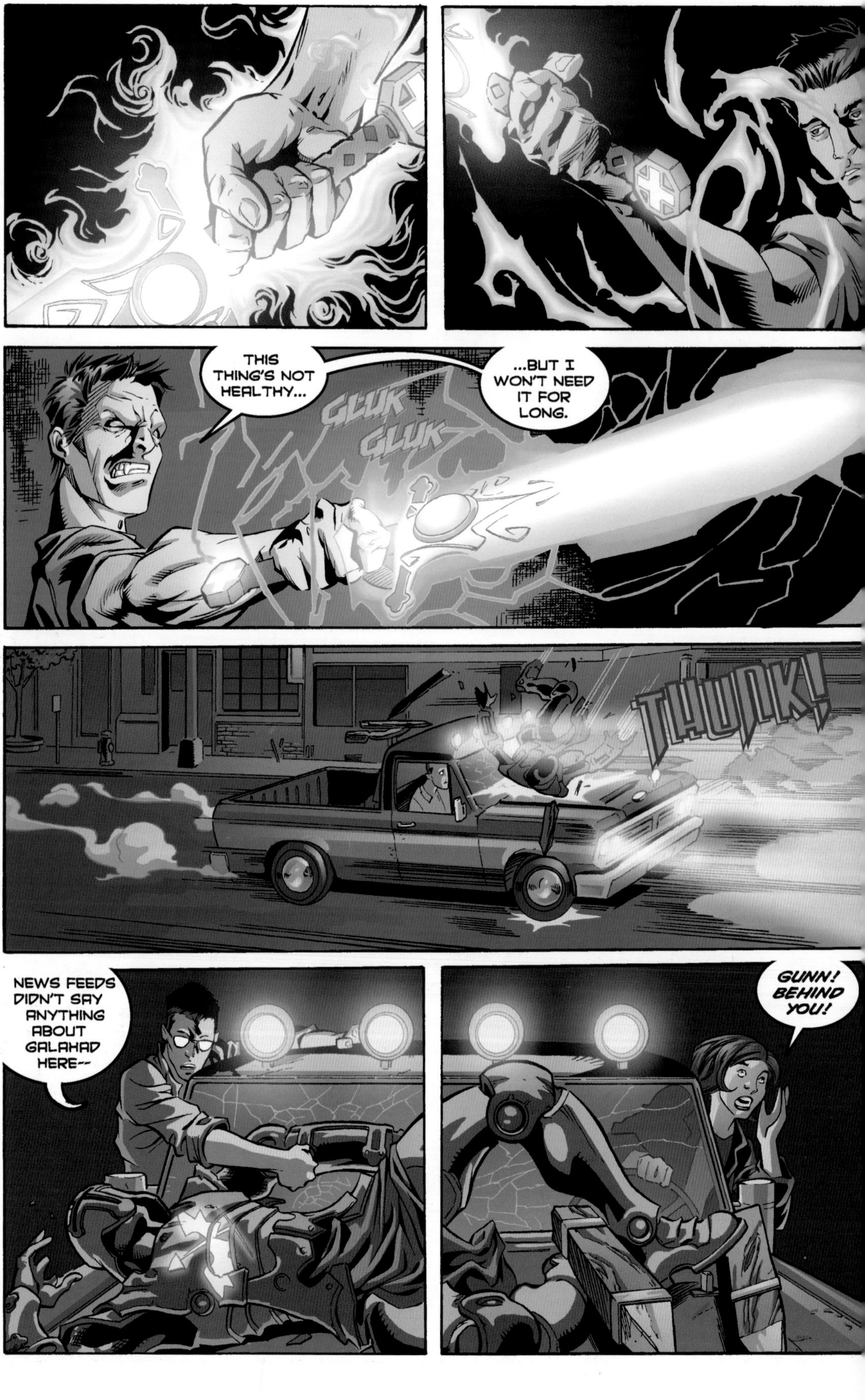
THIS THING'S NOT HEALTHY...
...BUT I WON'T NEED IT FOR LONG.
GLUK GLUK
THUNK!
NEWS FEEDS DIDN'T SAY ANYTHING ABOUT GALAHAD HERE--
GUNN! BEHIND YOU!

DID I GET IT?
GLUK
GLUK
GLORCH

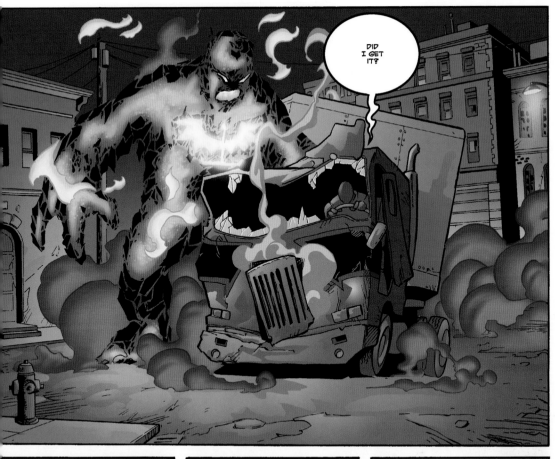

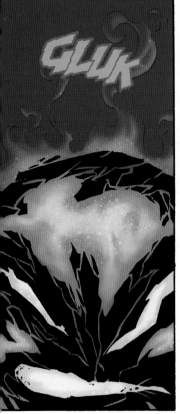

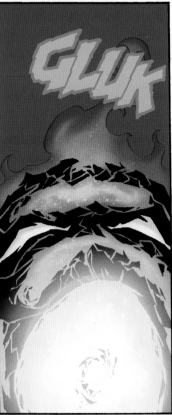

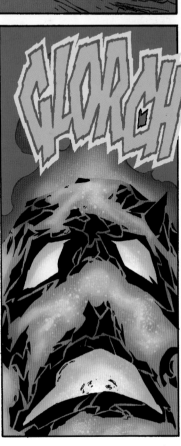

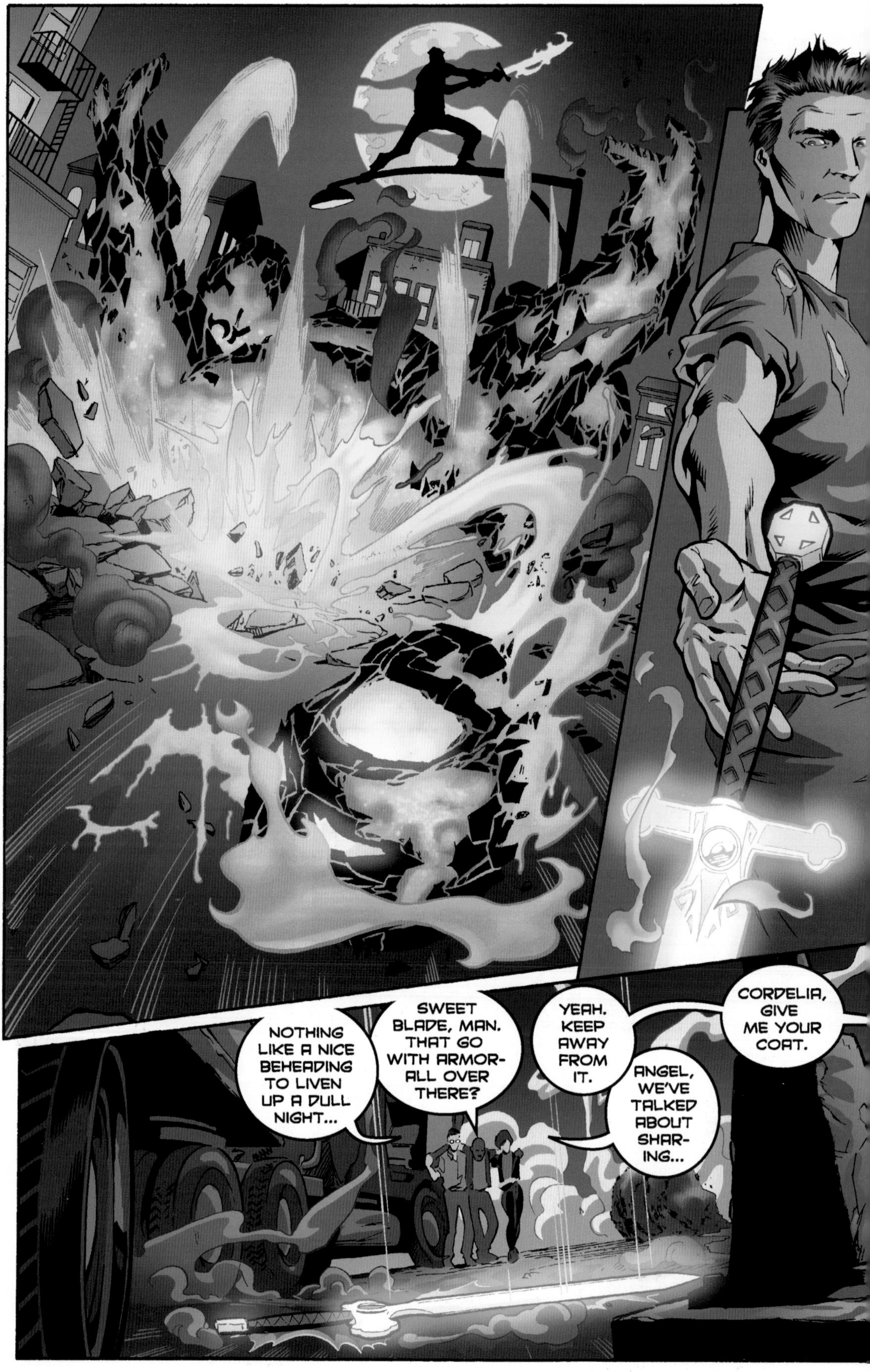

NOTHING LIKE A NICE BEHEADING TO LIVEN UP A DULL NIGHT...
SWEET BLADE, MAN. THAT GO WITH ARMOR-ALL OVER THERE?
YEAH. KEEP AWAY FROM IT.
CORDELIA, GIVE ME YOUR COAT.
ANGEL, WE'VE TALKED ABOUT SHAR-ING...

YOU KNOW THAT'S DRY CLEAN ONLY...

WHO ARE THESE GUYS, WESLEY?

TO BE HONEST I'VE NEVER SEEN THEM BEFORE. THEY'RE AN UNLIKELY DUO TO SAY THE LEAST--

THERE WERE THREE.

THREE?

YEAH, SOME KIND OF HALF-SERPENT HALF-SUPERMODEL. ALMOST KILLED ME, TILL HER PARTNERS SHOWED UP TO ALMOST KILL ME FOR HER.

I'M QUITE CERTAIN I WOULD REMEMBER RUNNING INTO SOMETHING LIKE THAT. NOR DOES IT SEEM A LIKELY FIT FOR OUR PRESENT COMPANY.

OKAY, THEN...

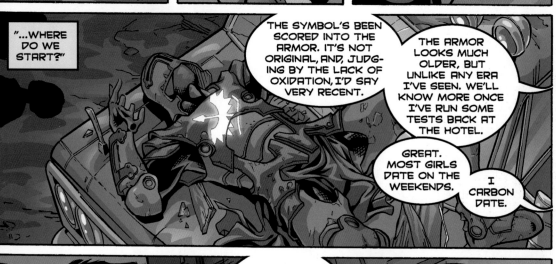

"...WHERE DO WE START?"

THE SYMBOL'S BEEN SCORED INTO THE ARMOR. IT'S NOT ORIGINAL, AND, JUDGING BY THE LACK OF OXIDATION, I'D SAY VERY RECENT.

THE ARMOR LOOKS MUCH OLDER, BUT UNLIKE ANY ERA I'VE SEEN. WE'LL KNOW MORE ONCE I'VE RUN SOME TESTS BACK AT THE HOTEL.

GREAT. MOST GIRLS DATE ON THE WEEKENDS.

I CARBON DATE.

I FEEL LIKE I'VE SEEN THE SYMBOL BEFORE. IT SEEMS TO CONTAIN A CHARACTER OF SOME SORT, PERHAPS KANJI. MY ASIAN LANGUAGES ARE A LITTLE RUSTY BUT--

CHINESE. IT MEANS "PERFECT."

OH.

HELL.

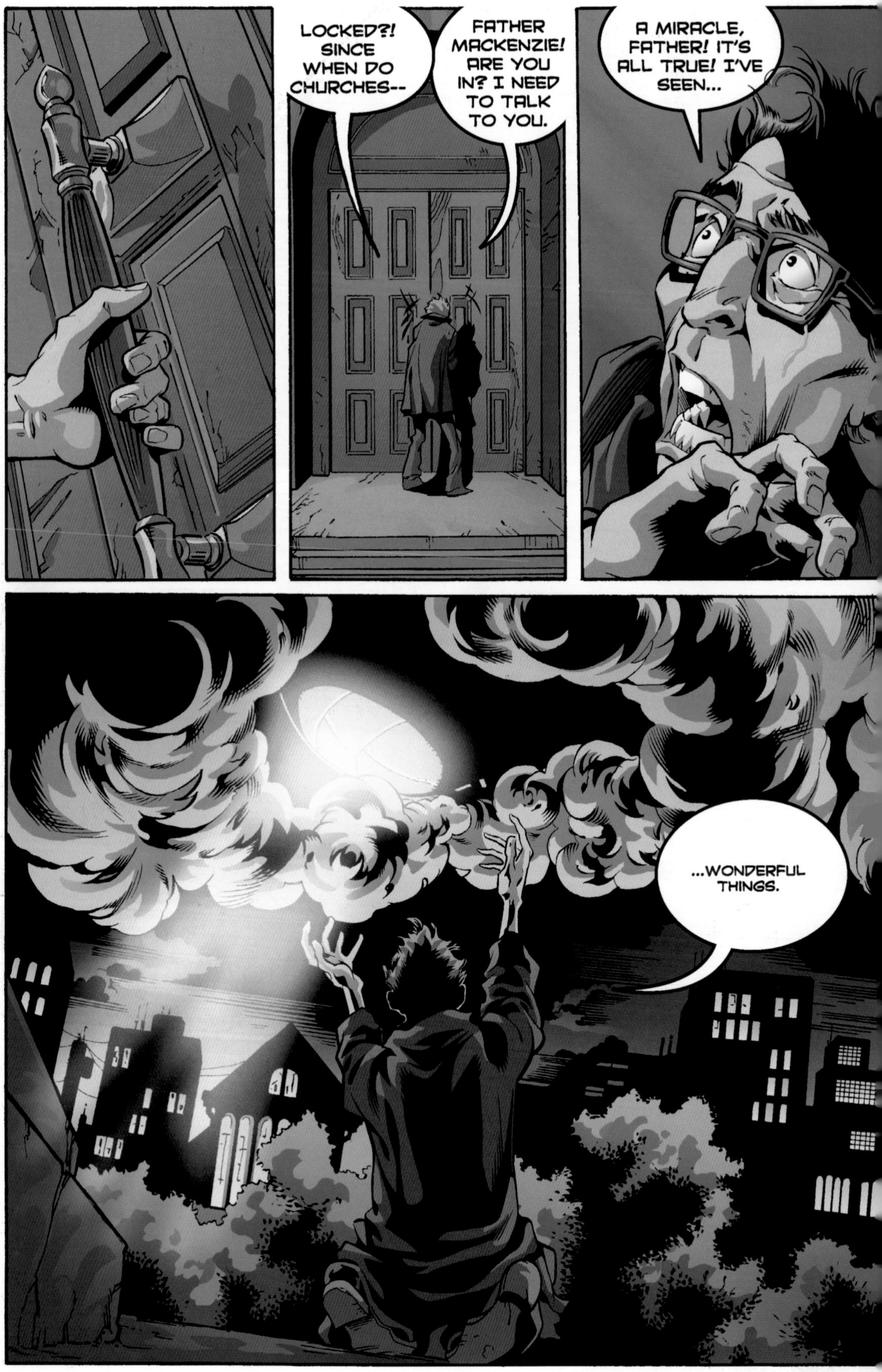
LOCKED?! SINCE WHEN DO CHURCHES--
FATHER MACKENZIE! ARE YOU IN? I NEED TO TALK TO YOU.
A MIRACLE, FATHER! IT'S ALL TRUE! I'VE SEEN...
...WONDERFUL THINGS.

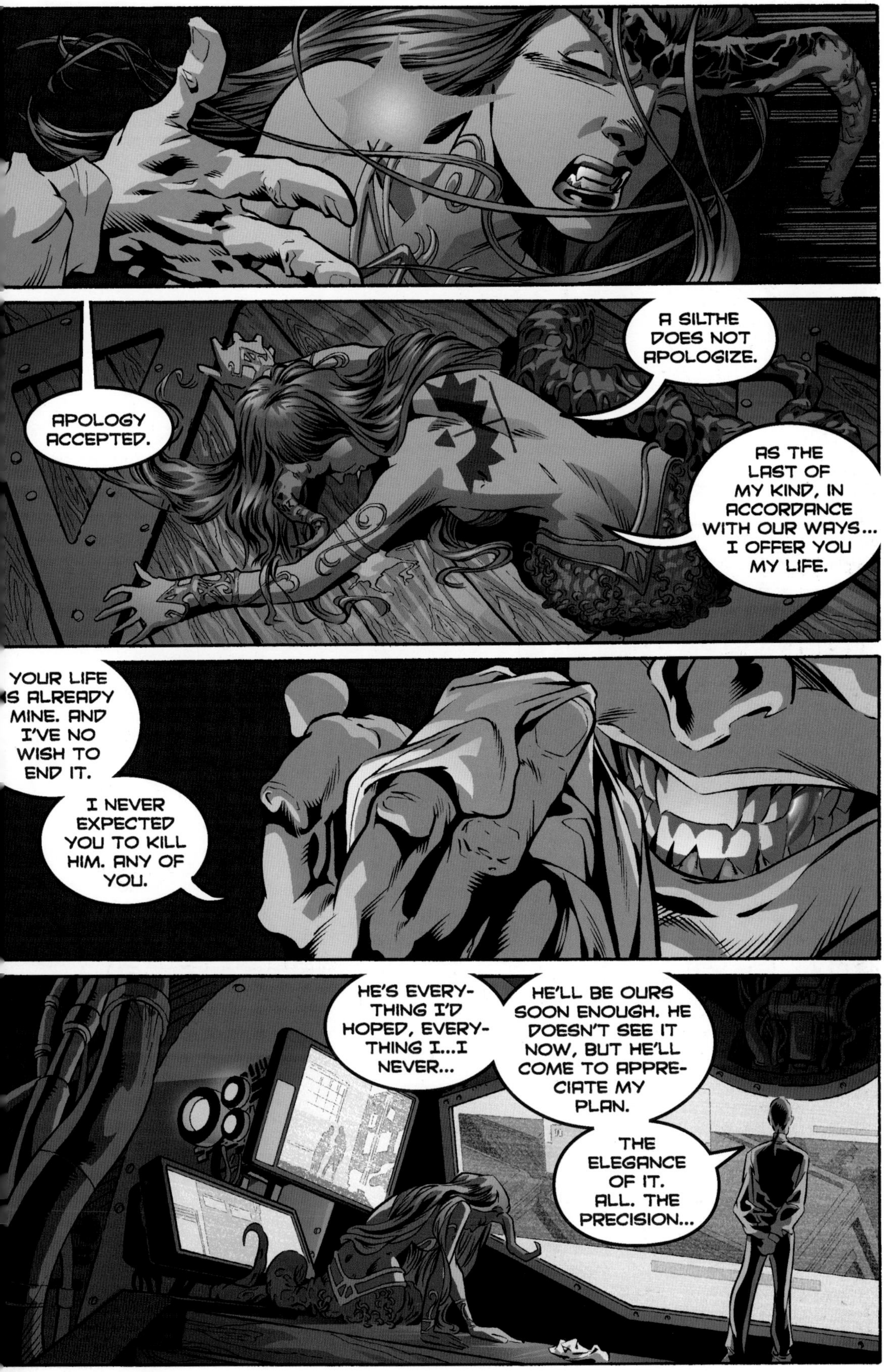
APOLOGY ACCEPTED.
A SILTHE DOES NOT APOLOGIZE.
AS THE LAST OF MY KIND, IN ACCORDANCE WITH OUR WAYS... I OFFER YOU MY LIFE.
YOUR LIFE IS ALREADY MINE. AND I'VE NO WISH TO END IT.
I NEVER EXPECTED YOU TO KILL HIM. ANY OF YOU.
HE'S EVERY-THING I'D HOPED, EVERY-THING I...I NEVER...
HE'LL BE OURS SOON ENOUGH. HE DOESN'T SEE IT NOW, BUT HE'LL COME TO APPRE-CIATE MY PLAN.
THE ELEGANCE OF IT. ALL. THE PRECISION...

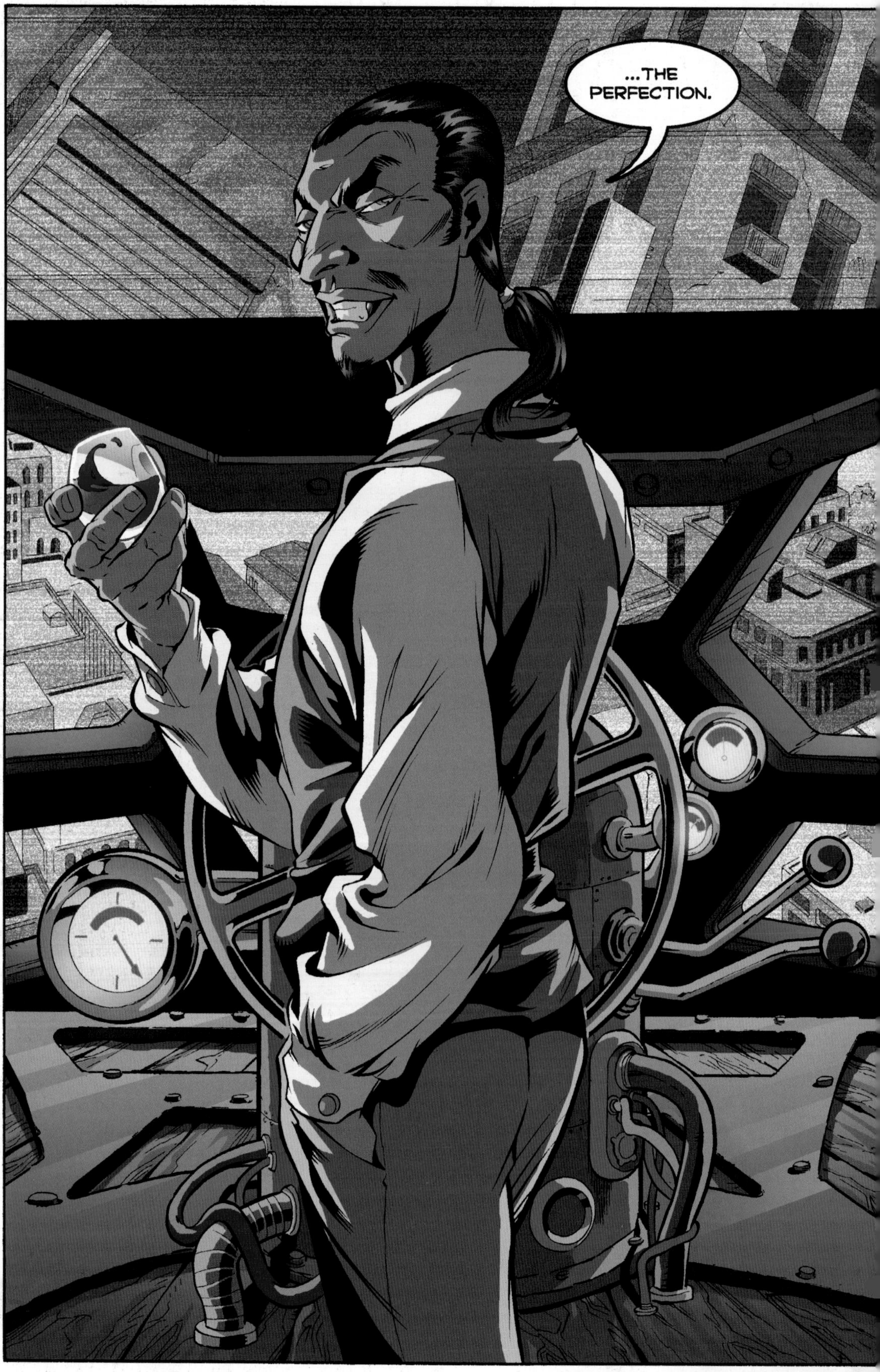
...THE PERFECTION.

Three

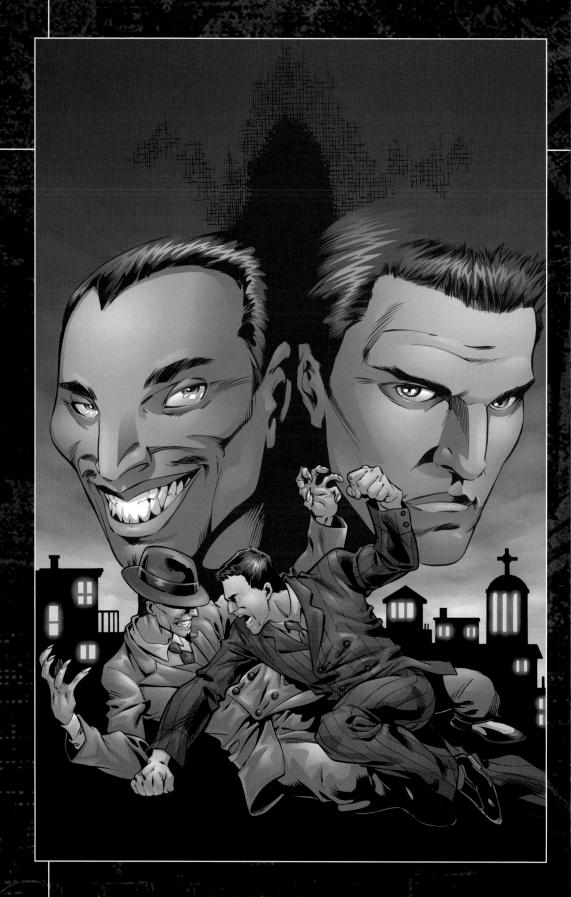

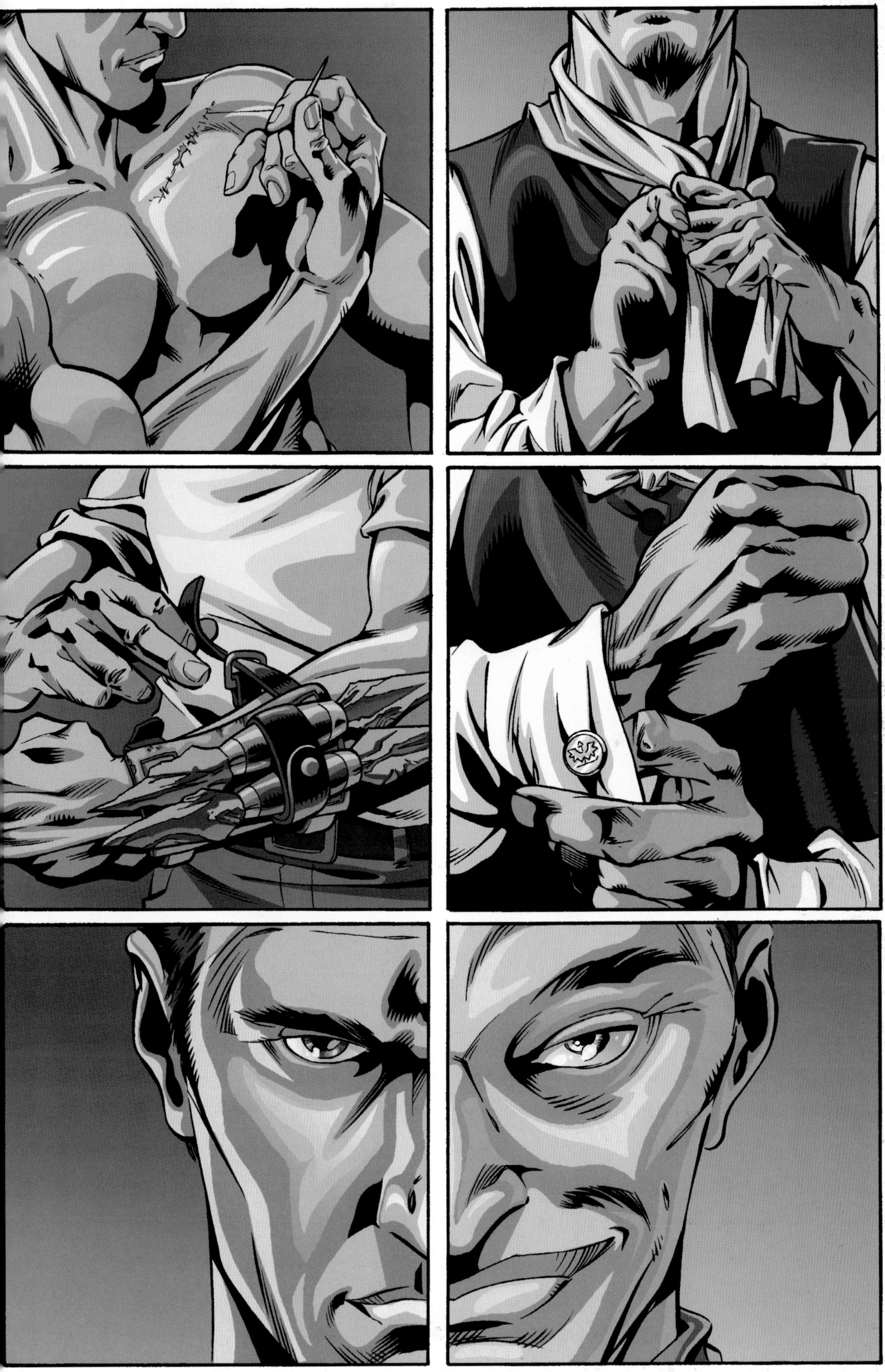

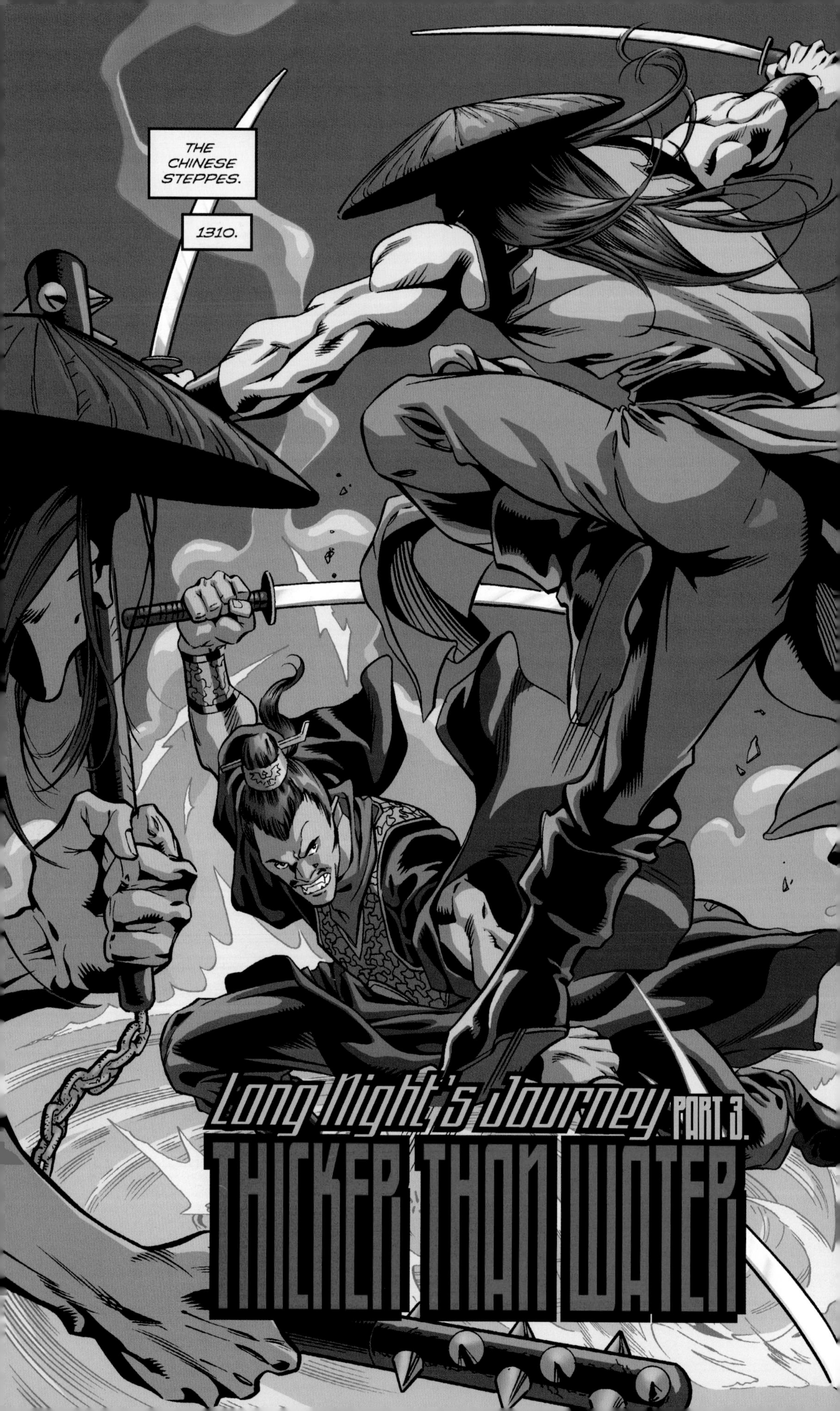

THE CHINESE STEPPES.
1310.
Long Night's Journey PART 3.
THICKER THAN WATER

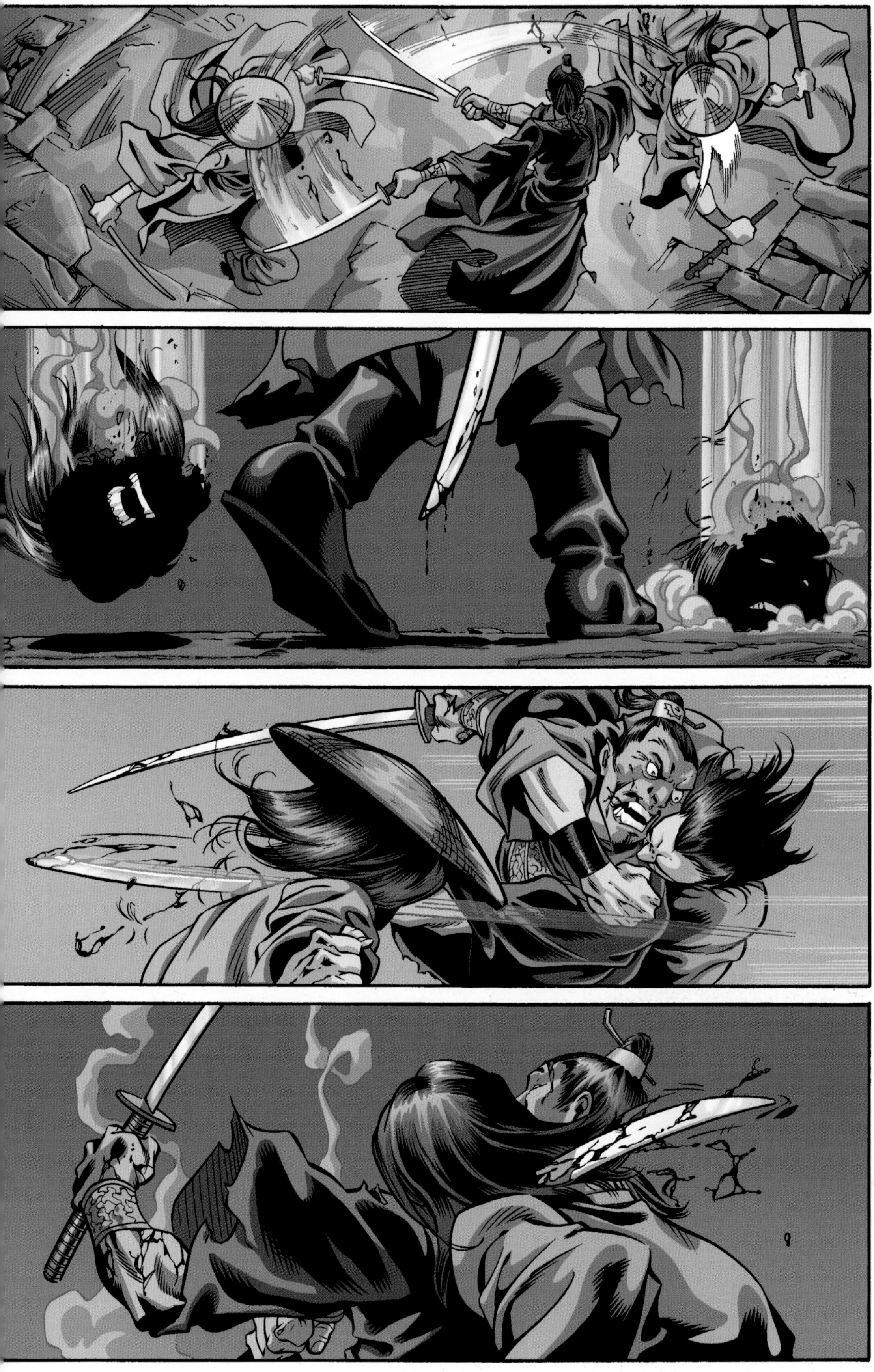

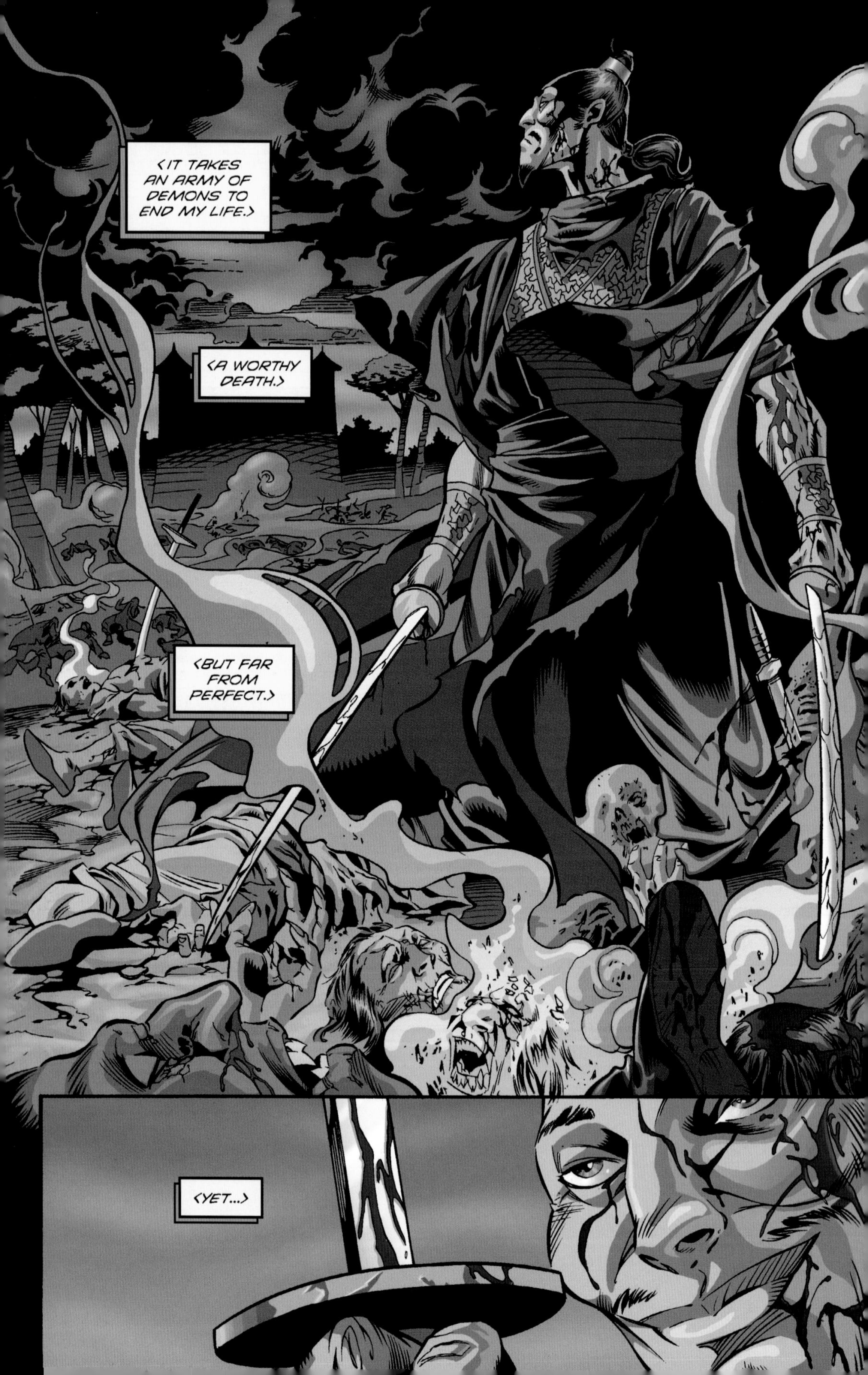
<IT TAKES AN ARMY OF DEMONS TO END MY LIFE.>
<A WORTHY DEATH.>
<BUT FAR FROM PERFECT.>
<YET...>

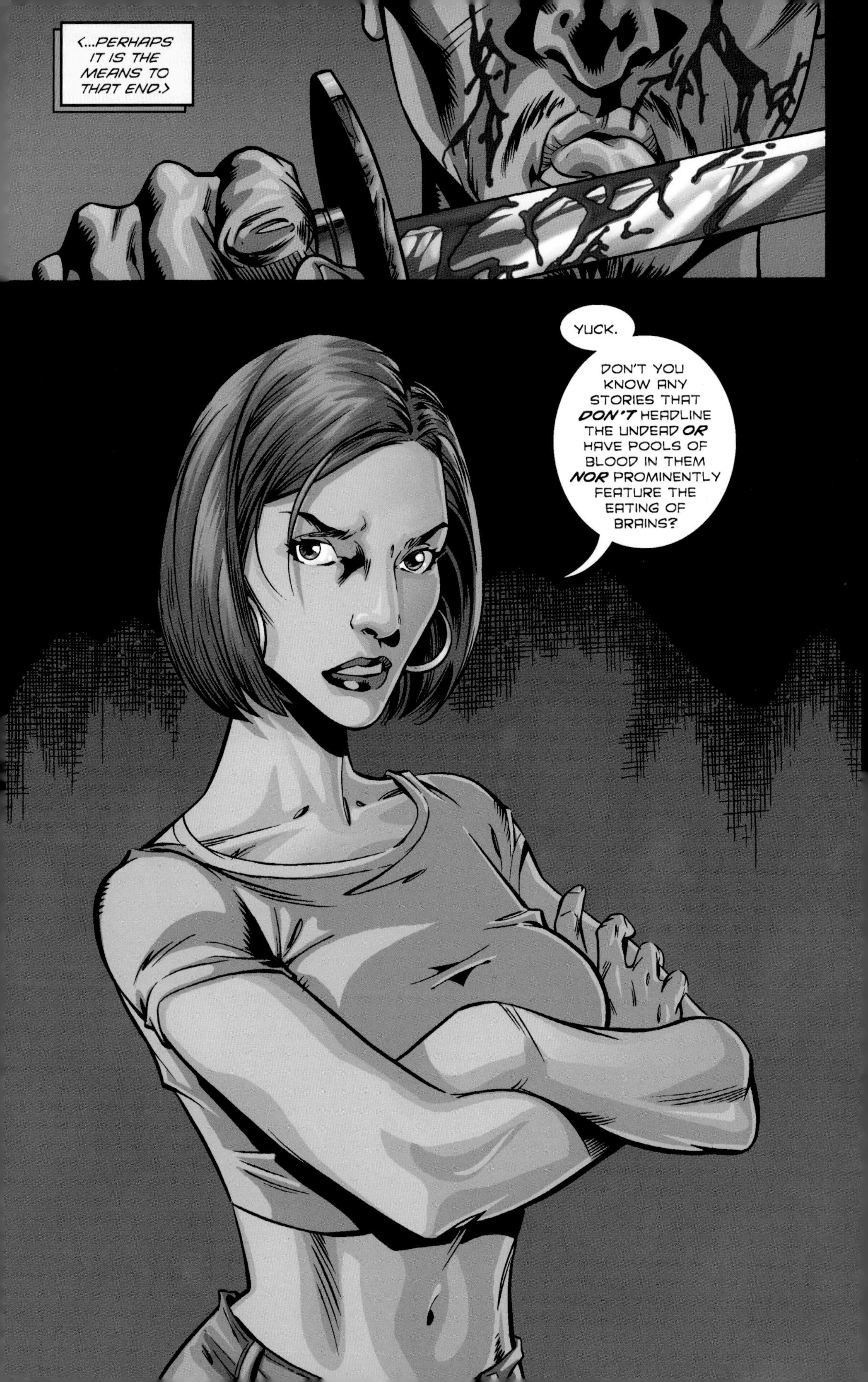
<...PERHAPS IT IS THE MEANS TO THAT END.>
YUCK.
DON'T YOU KNOW ANY STORIES THAT DON'T HEADLINE THE UNDEAD OR HAVE POOLS OF BLOOD IN THEM NOR PROMINENTLY FEATURE THE EATING OF BRAINS?

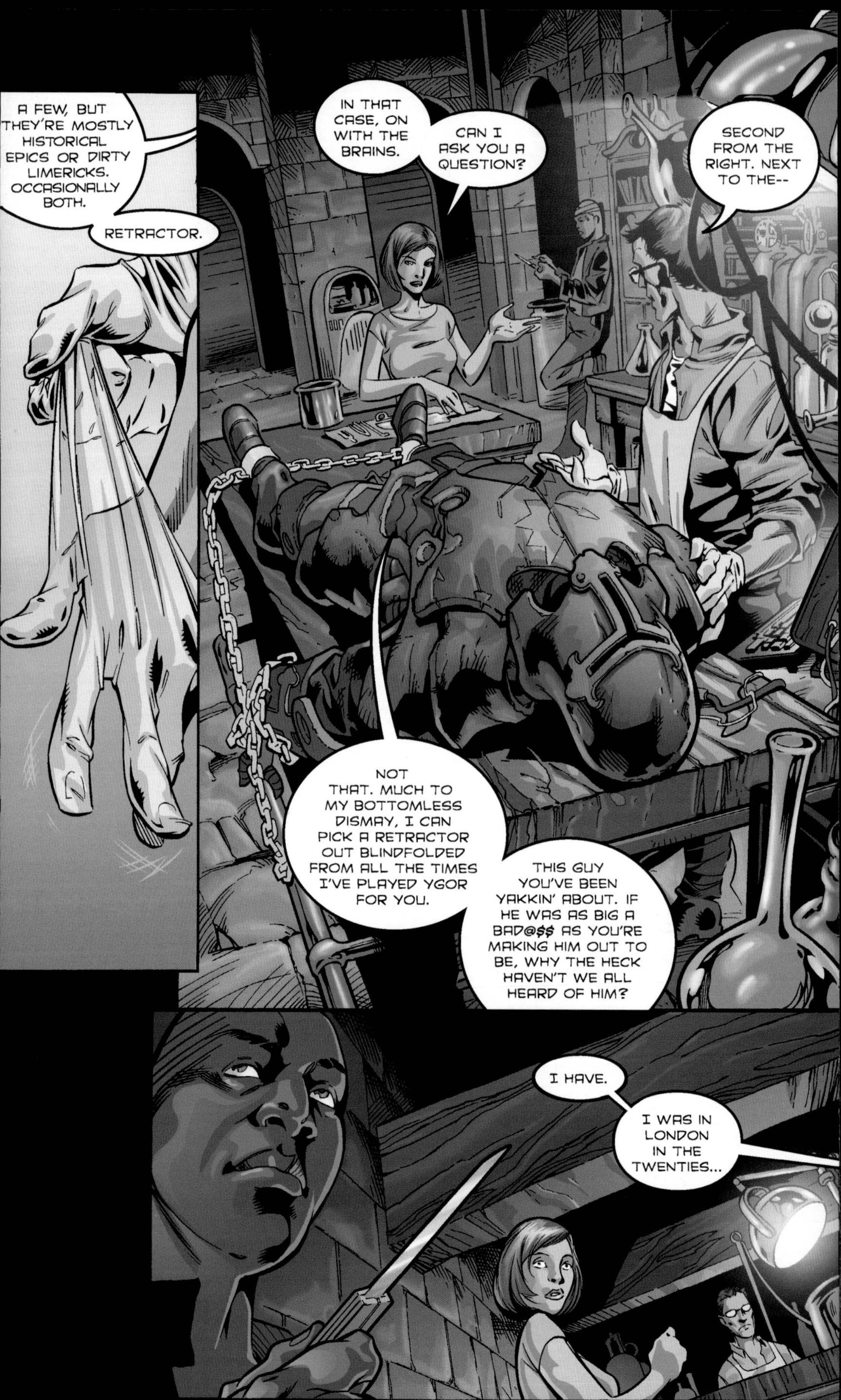
A FEW, BUT THEY'RE MOSTLY HISTORICAL EPICS OR DIRTY LIMERICKS. OCCASIONALLY BOTH.
RETRACTOR.
IN THAT CASE, ON WITH THE BRAINS.
CAN I ASK YOU A QUESTION?
SECOND FROM THE RIGHT. NEXT TO THE--
NOT THAT. MUCH TO MY BOTTOMLESS DISMAY, I CAN PICK A RETRACTOR OUT BLINDFOLDED FROM ALL THE TIMES I'VE PLAYED YGOR FOR YOU.
THIS GUY YOU'VE BEEN YAKKIN' ABOUT. IF HE WAS AS BIG A BAD@$$ AS YOU'RE MAKING HIM OUT TO BE, WHY THE HECK HAVEN'T WE ALL HEARD OF HIM?
I HAVE.
I WAS IN LONDON IN THE TWENTIES...

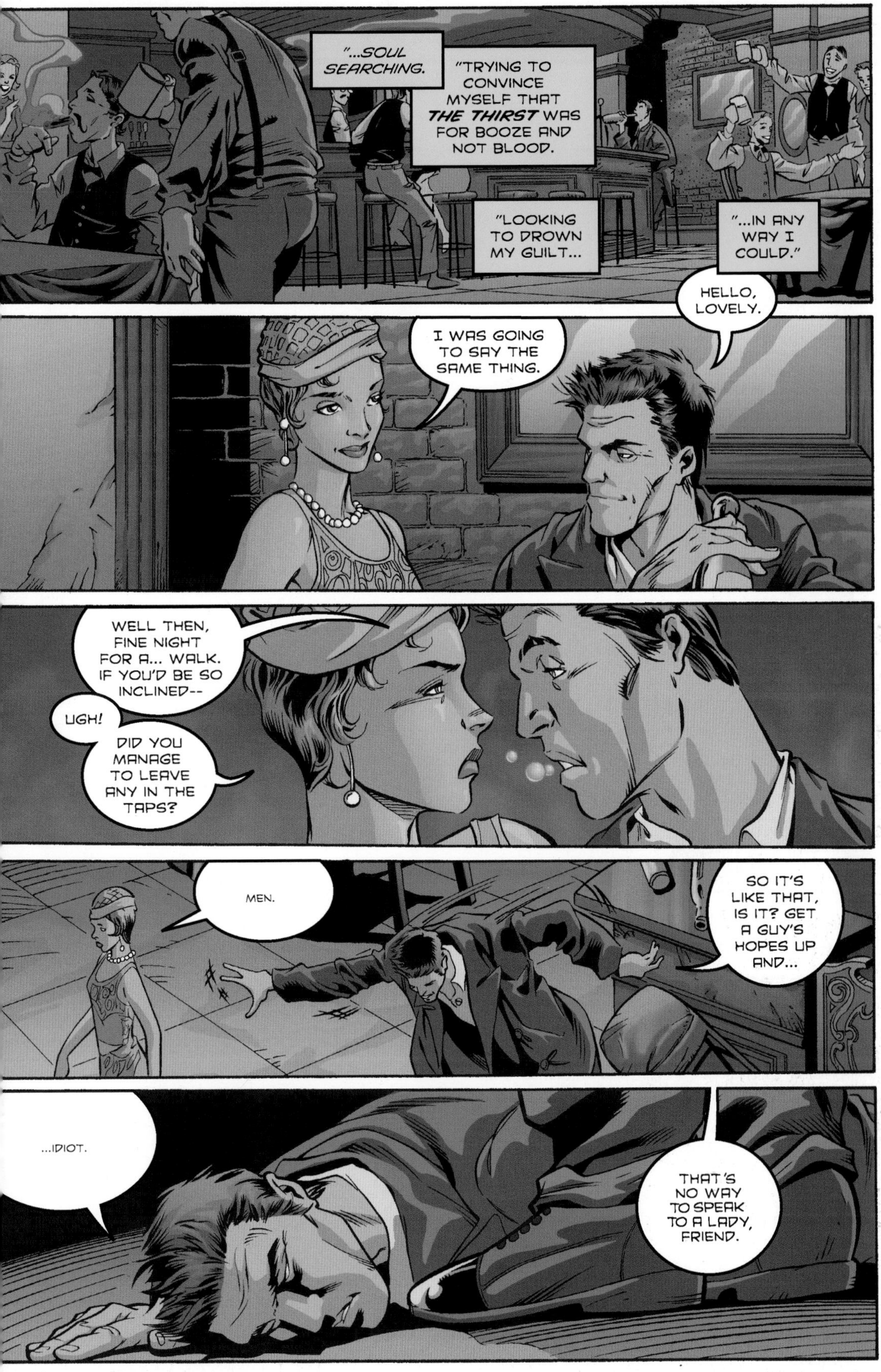
"...SOUL SEARCHING.
"TRYING TO CONVINCE MYSELF THAT THE THIRST WAS FOR BOOZE AND NOT BLOOD.
"LOOKING TO DROWN MY GUILT...
"...IN ANY WAY I COULD."
HELLO, LOVELY.
I WAS GOING TO SAY THE SAME THING.
WELL THEN, FINE NIGHT FOR A... WALK. IF YOU'D BE SO INCLINED--
UGH!
DID YOU MANAGE TO LEAVE ANY IN THE TAPS?
SO IT'S LIKE THAT, IS IT? GET A GUY'S HOPES UP AND...
MEN.
...IDIOT.
THAT'S NO WAY TO SPEAK TO A LADY, FRIEND.

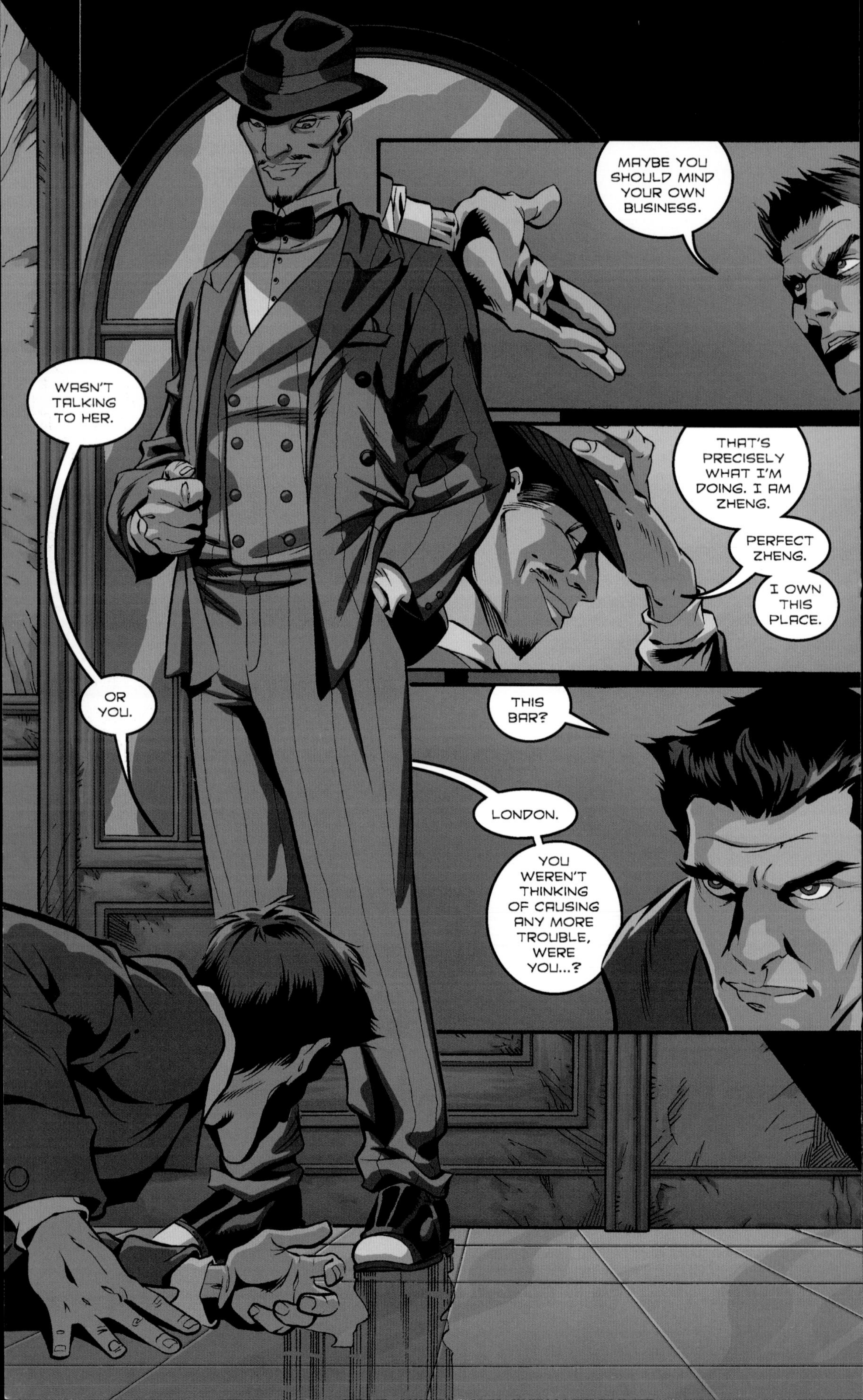

WASN'T TALKING TO HER.
OR YOU.
MAYBE YOU SHOULD MIND YOUR OWN BUSINESS.
THAT'S PRECISELY WHAT I'M DOING. I AM ZHENG.
PERFECT ZHENG.
I OWN THIS PLACE.
THIS BAR?
LONDON.
YOU WEREN'T THINKING OF CAUSING ANY MORE TROUBLE, WERE YOU...?

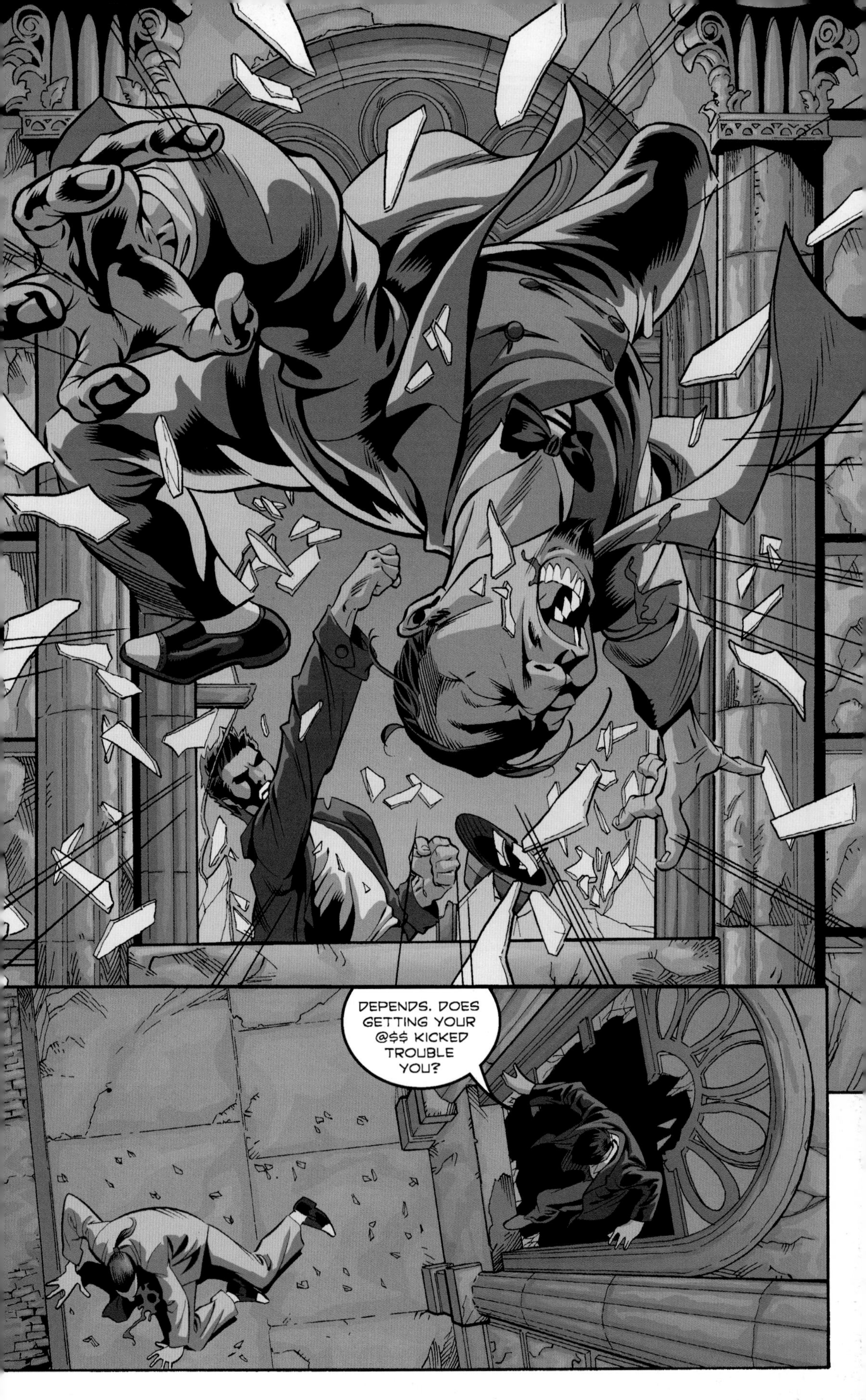
DEPENDS. DOES GETTING YOUR @$$ KICKED TROUBLE YOU?

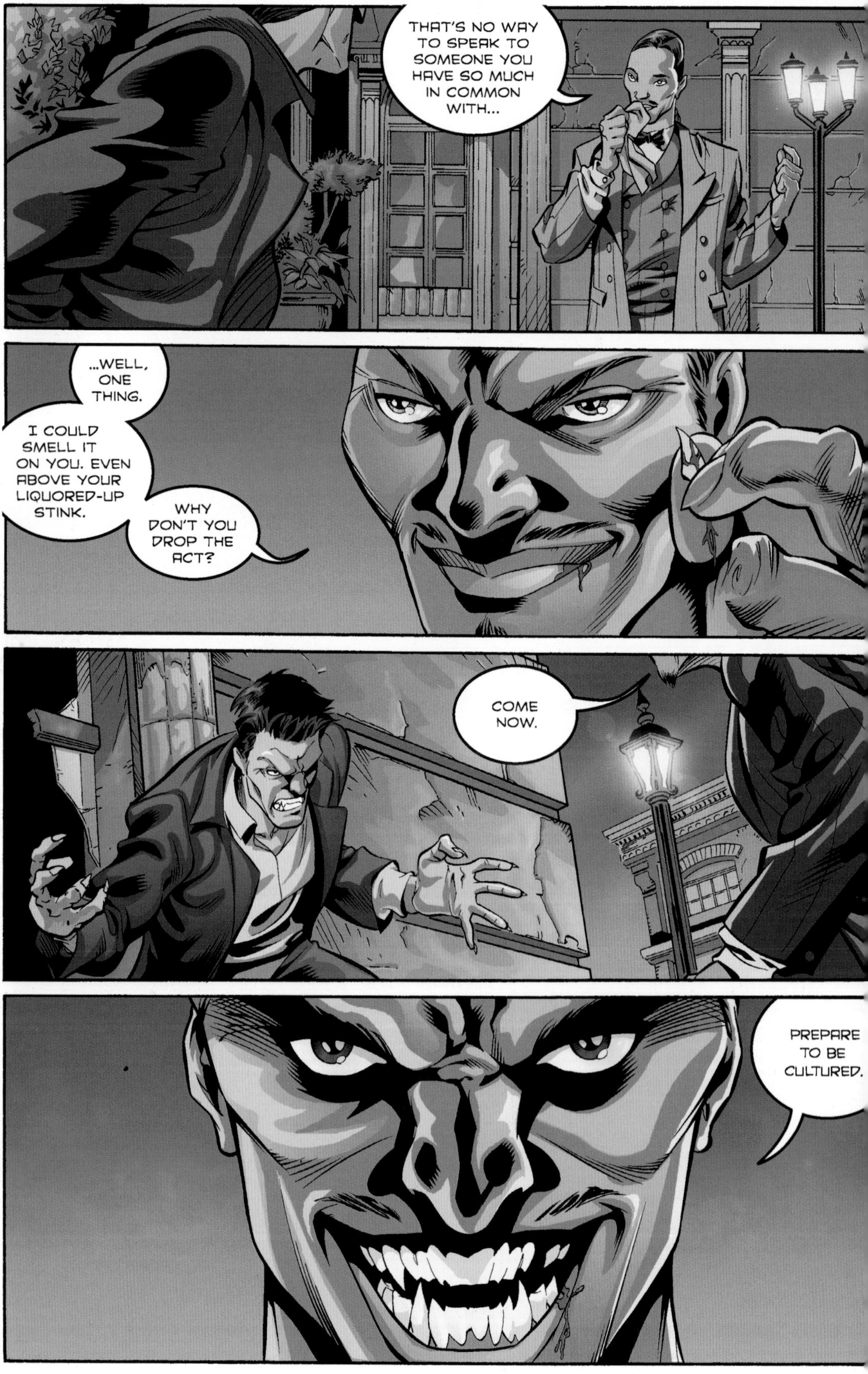
THAT'S NO WAY TO SPEAK TO SOMEONE YOU HAVE SO MUCH IN COMMON WITH...
...WELL, ONE THING.
I COULD SMELL IT ON YOU. EVEN ABOVE YOUR LIQUORED-UP STINK.
WHY DON'T YOU DROP THE ACT?
COME NOW.
PREPARE TO BE CULTURED.

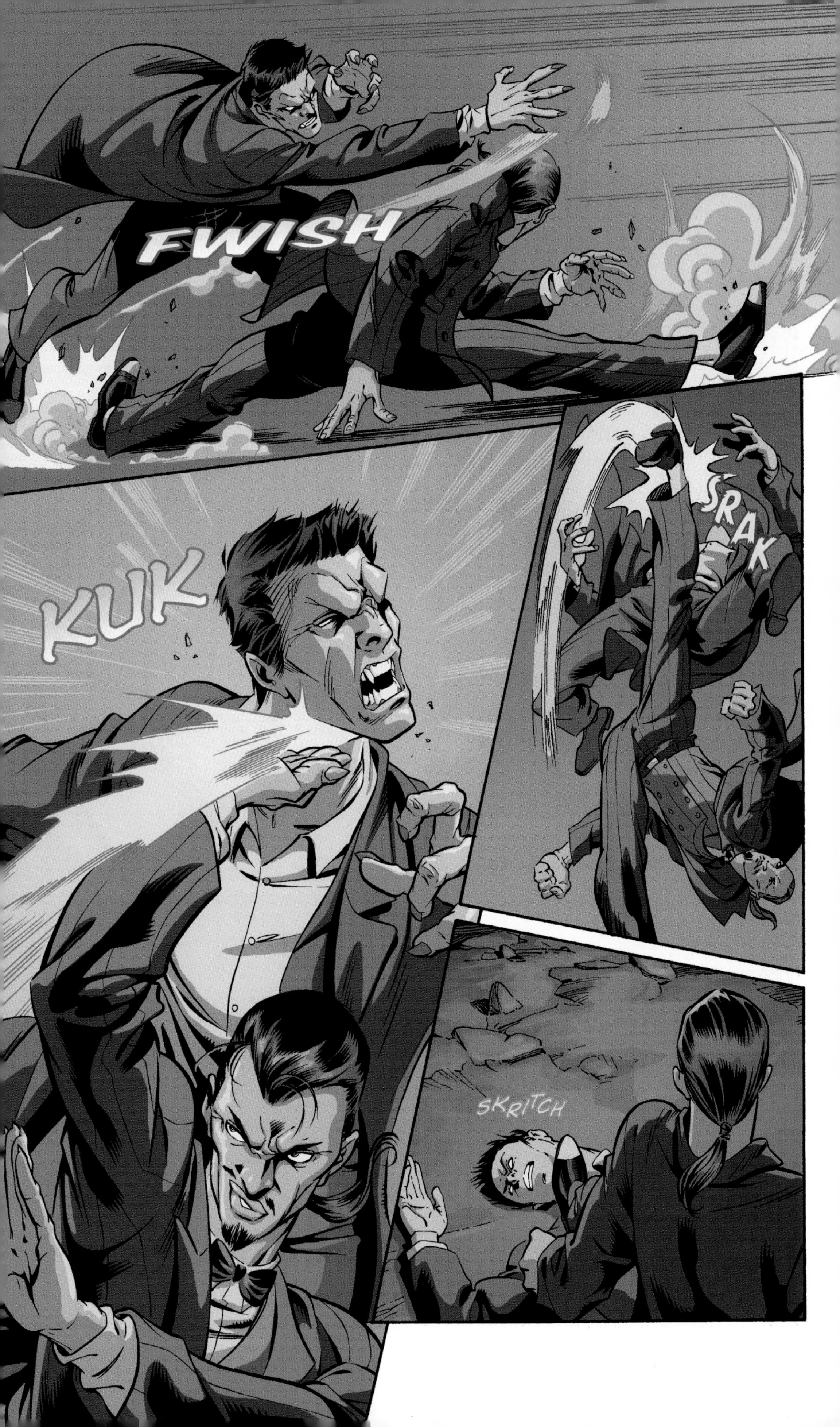
FWISH
SRAK
KUK
SKRITCH

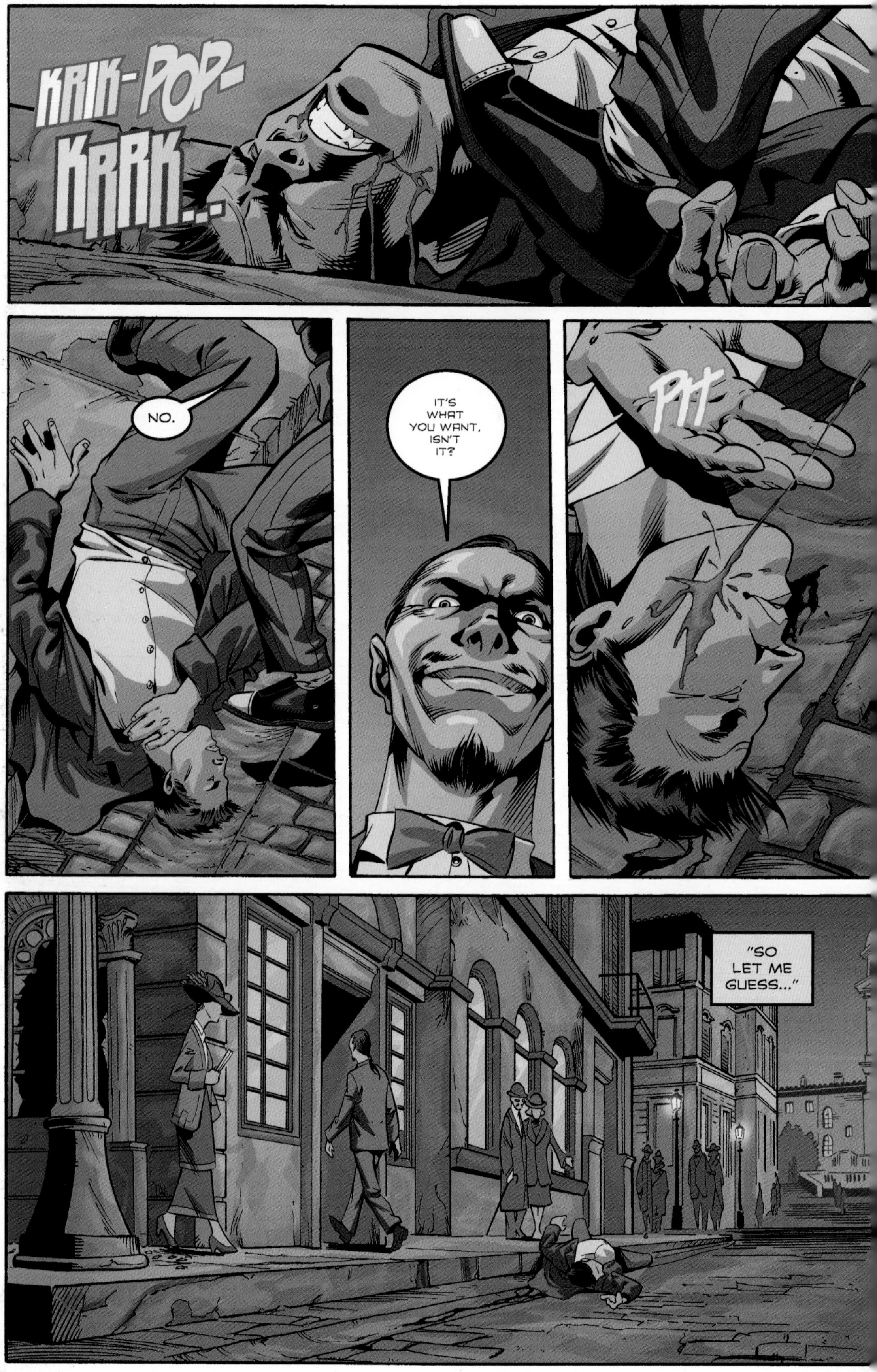
KRIK-POP-KRRK...
NO.
IT'S WHAT YOU WANT, ISN'T IT?
PH
"SO LET ME GUESS..."

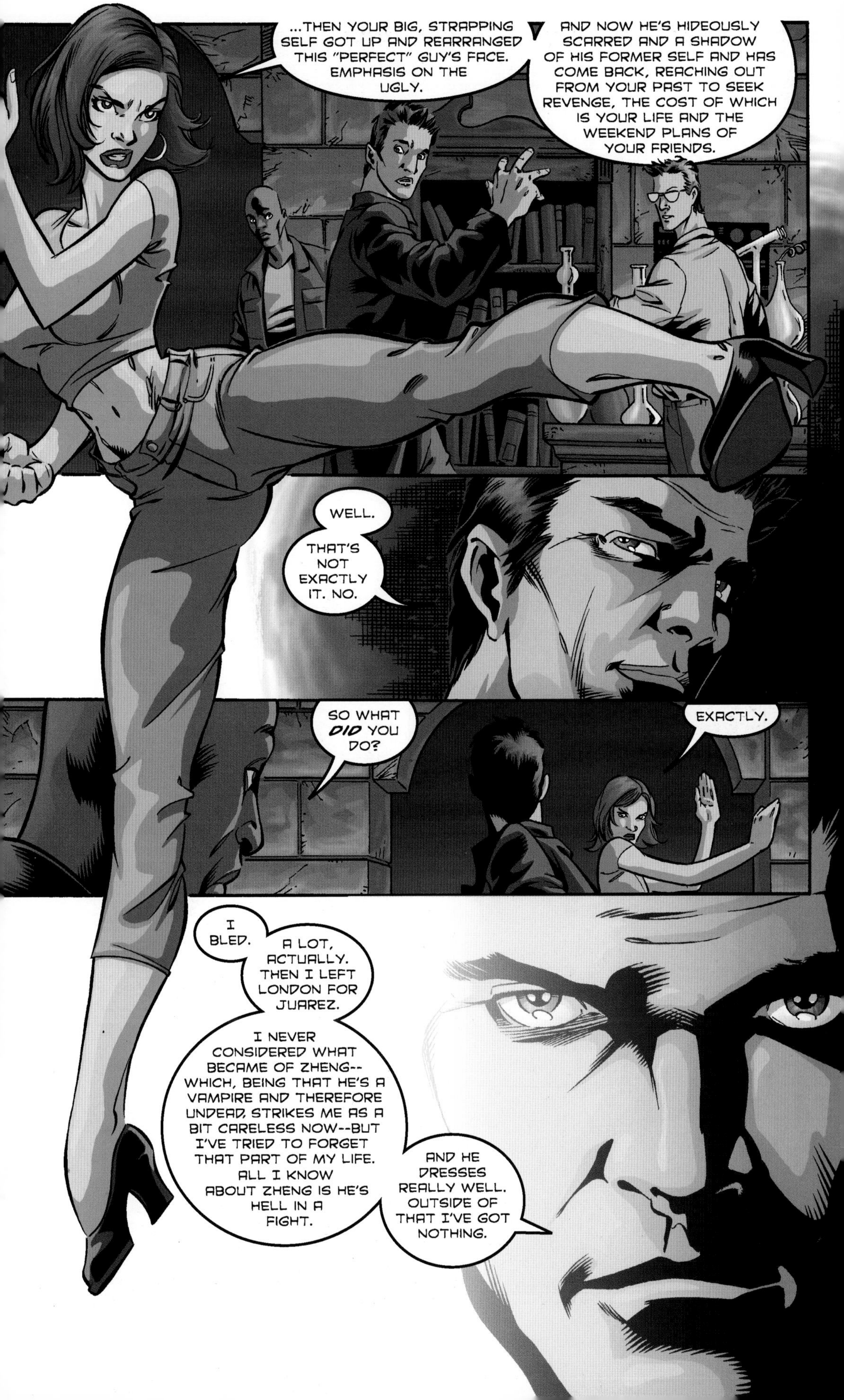
...THEN YOUR BIG, STRAPPING SELF GOT UP AND REARRANGED THIS "PERFECT" GUY'S FACE. EMPHASIS ON THE UGLY.
AND NOW HE'S HIDEOUSLY SCARRED AND A SHADOW OF HIS FORMER SELF AND HAS COME BACK, REACHING OUT FROM YOUR PAST TO SEEK REVENGE, THE COST OF WHICH IS YOUR LIFE AND THE WEEKEND PLANS OF YOUR FRIENDS.
WELL.
THAT'S NOT EXACTLY IT. NO.
SO WHAT *DID* YOU DO?
EXACTLY.
I BLED.
A LOT, ACTUALLY. THEN I LEFT LONDON FOR JUAREZ.
I NEVER CONSIDERED WHAT BECAME OF ZHENG-- WHICH, BEING THAT HE'S A VAMPIRE AND THEREFORE UNDEAD, STRIKES ME AS A BIT CARELESS NOW--BUT I'VE TRIED TO FORGET THAT PART OF MY LIFE. ALL I KNOW ABOUT ZHENG IS HE'S HELL IN A FIGHT.
AND HE DRESSES REALLY WELL. OUTSIDE OF THAT I'VE GOT NOTHING.

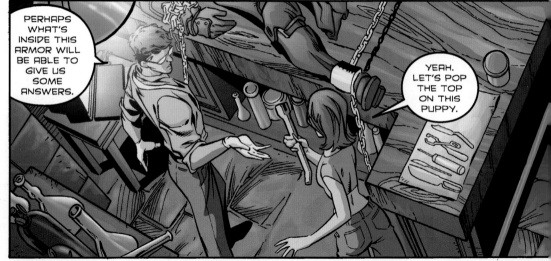

PERHAPS WHAT'S INSIDE THIS ARMOR WILL BE ABLE TO GIVE US SOME ANSWERS.

YEAH. LET'S POP THE TOP ON THIS PUPPY.

SHINK

CORDELIA.

GET THE BLOWTORCH.

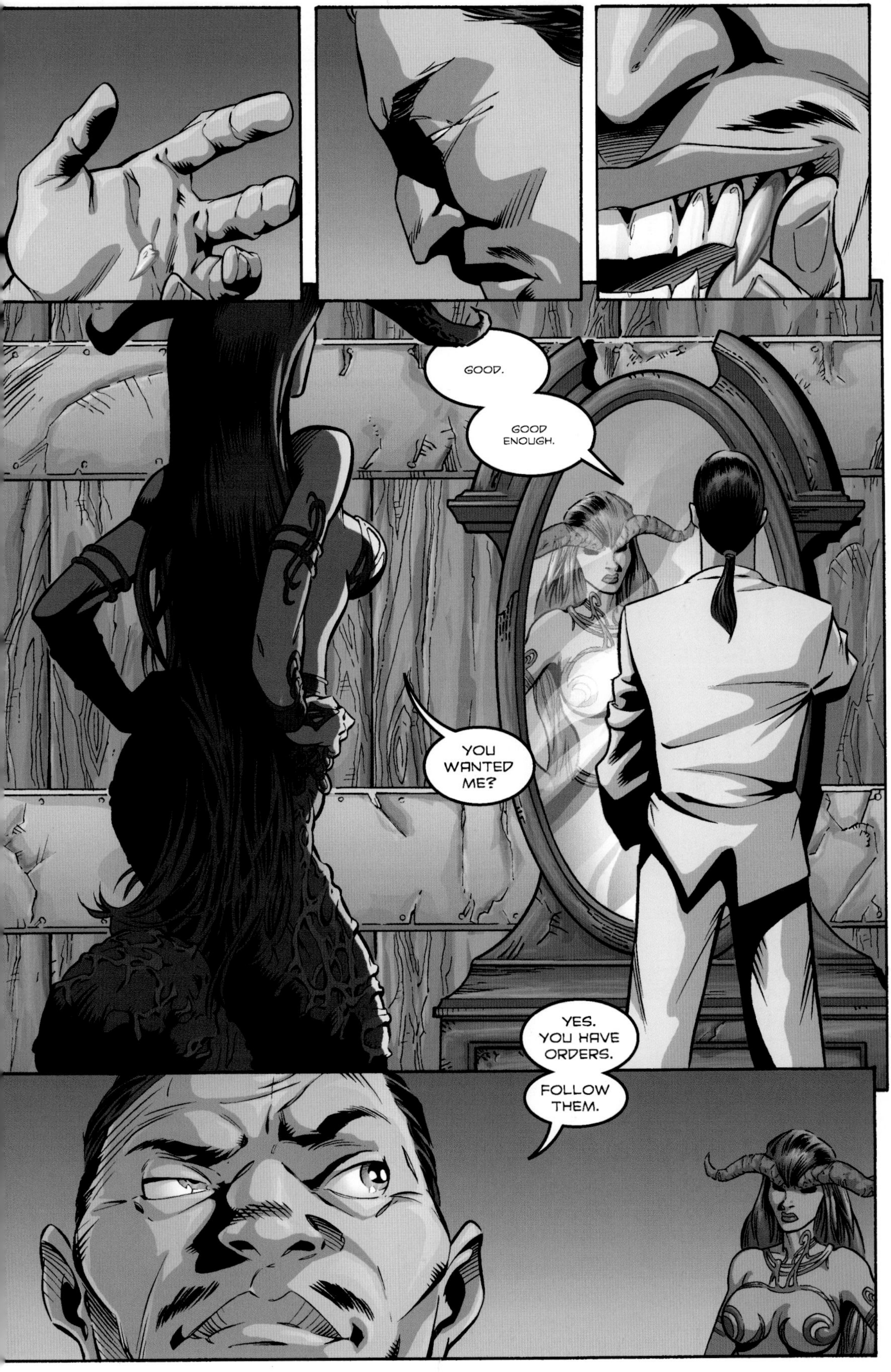
GOOD.
GOOD ENOUGH.
YOU WANTED ME?
YES. YOU HAVE ORDERS.
FOLLOW THEM.

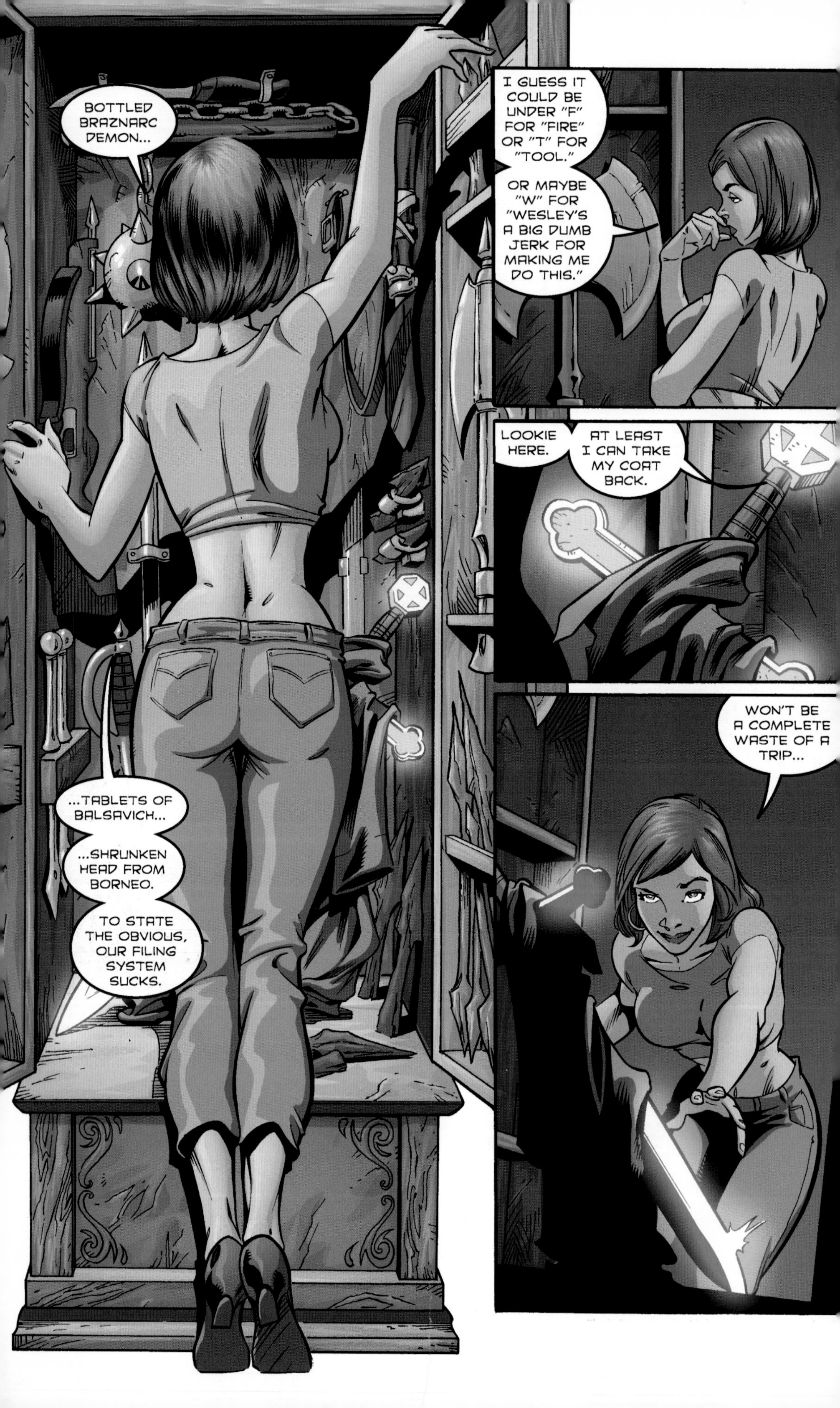

BOTTLED BRAZNARC DEMON...
...TABLETS OF BALSAVICH...
...SHRUNKEN HEAD FROM BORNEO.
TO STATE THE OBVIOUS, OUR FILING SYSTEM SUCKS.
I GUESS IT COULD BE UNDER "F" FOR "FIRE" OR "T" FOR "TOOL."
OR MAYBE "W" FOR "WESLEY'S A BIG DUMB JERK FOR MAKING ME DO THIS."
LOOKIE HERE.
AT LEAST I CAN TAKE MY COAT BACK.
WON'T BE A COMPLETE WASTE OF A TRIP...

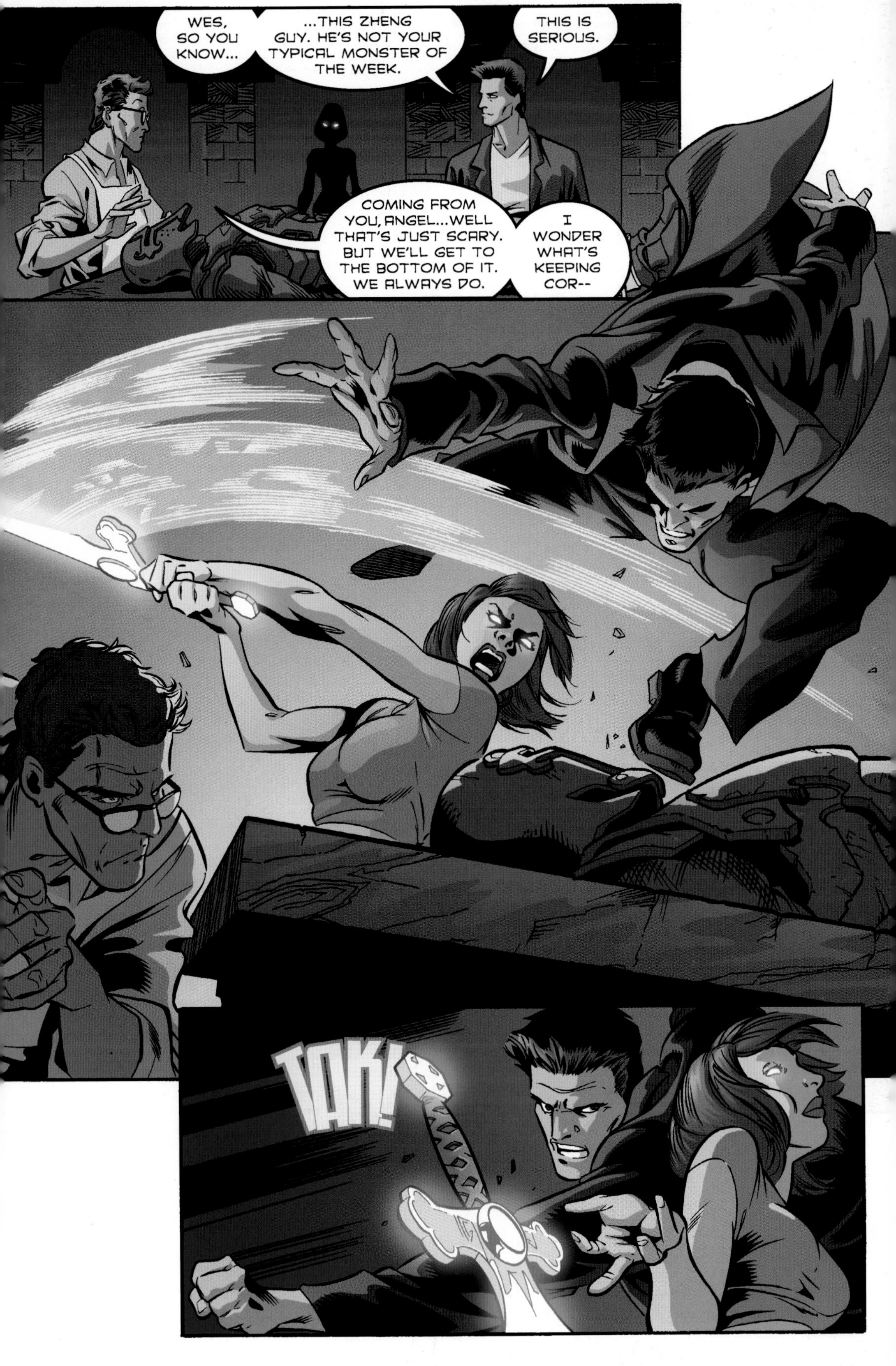

WES, SO YOU KNOW...
...THIS ZHENG GUY. HE'S NOT YOUR TYPICAL MONSTER OF THE WEEK.
THIS IS SERIOUS.
COMING FROM YOU, ANGEL...WELL THAT'S JUST SCARY. BUT WE'LL GET TO THE BOTTOM OF IT. WE ALWAYS DO.
I WONDER WHAT'S KEEPING COR--
TAK!

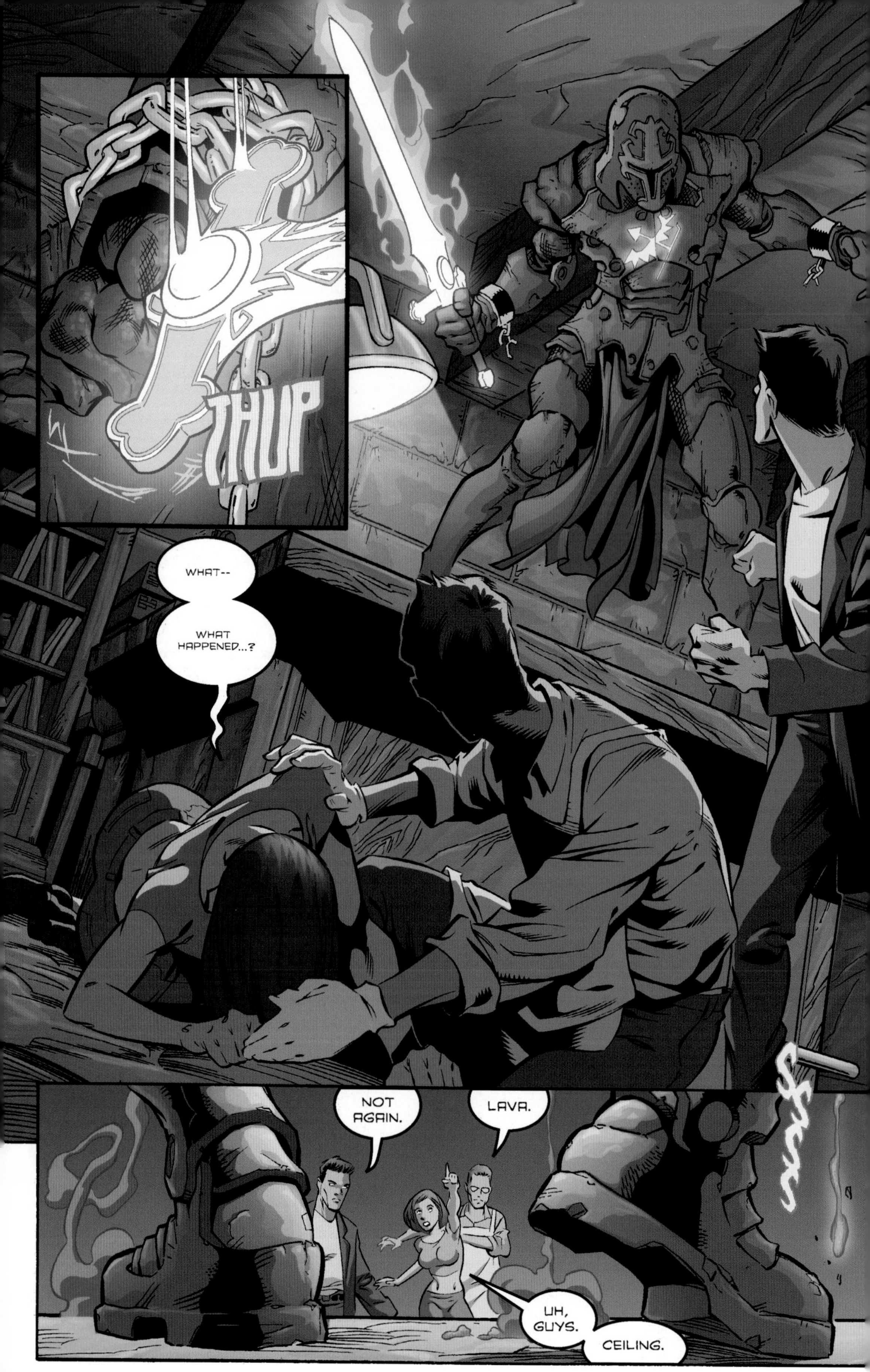
THUP
WHAT--
WHAT HAPPENED...?
NOT AGAIN.
LAVA.
UH, GUYS.
CEILING.

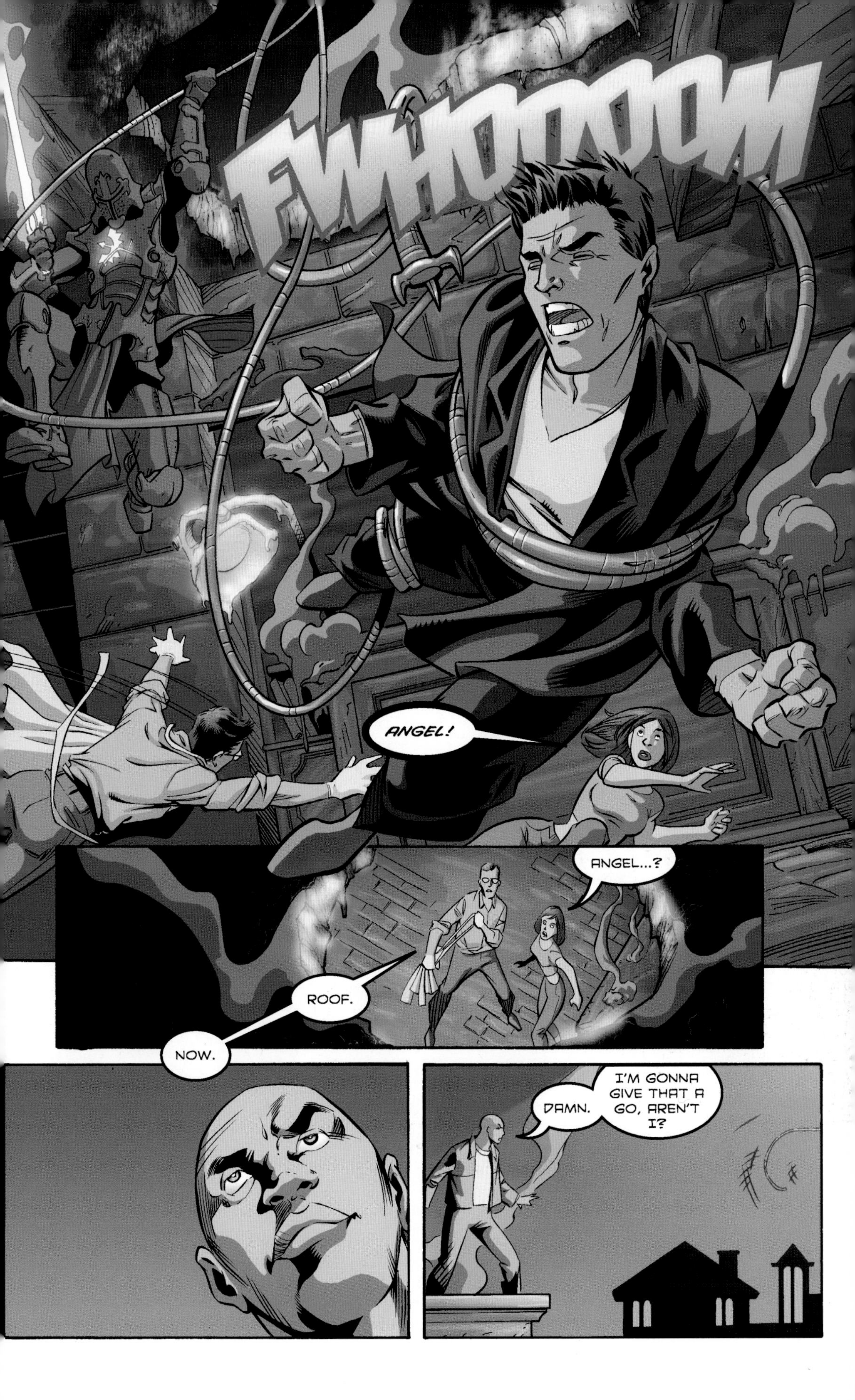
FWHOOOOM
ANGEL!
ANGEL...?
ROOF.
NOW.
DAMN.
I'M GONNA GIVE THAT A GO, AREN'T I?

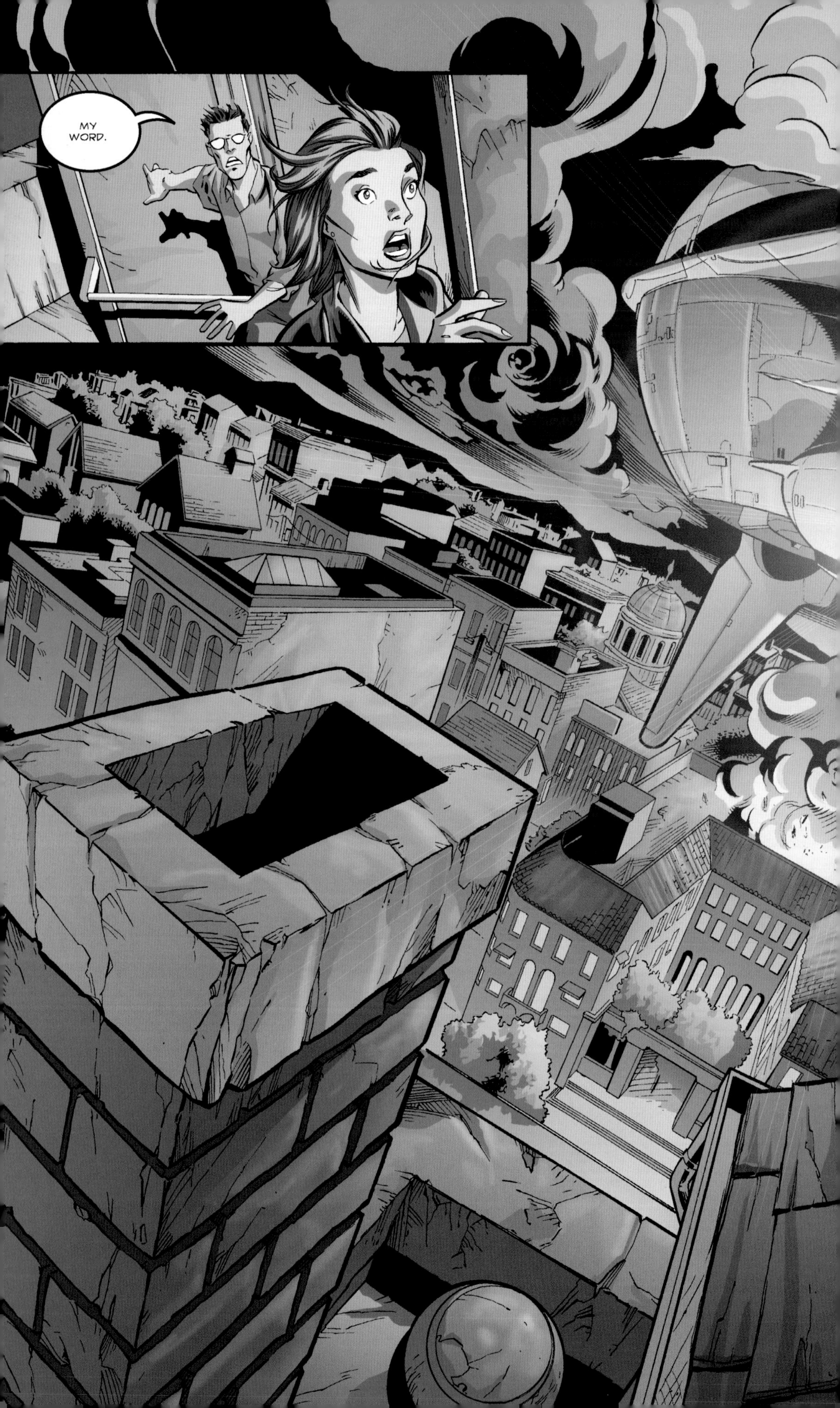
MY WORD.

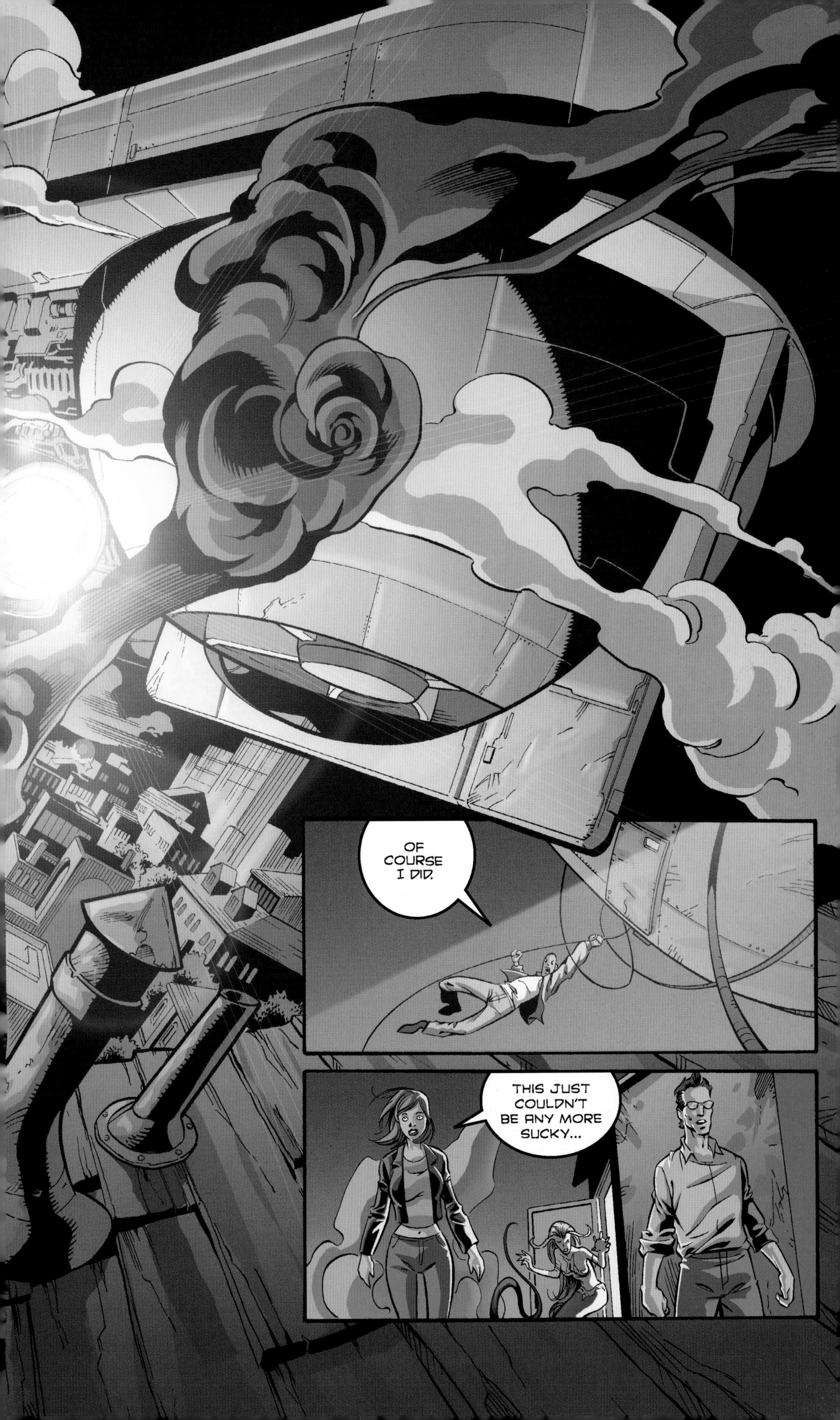
OF COURSE I DID.
THIS JUST COULDN'T BE ANY MORE SUCKY...

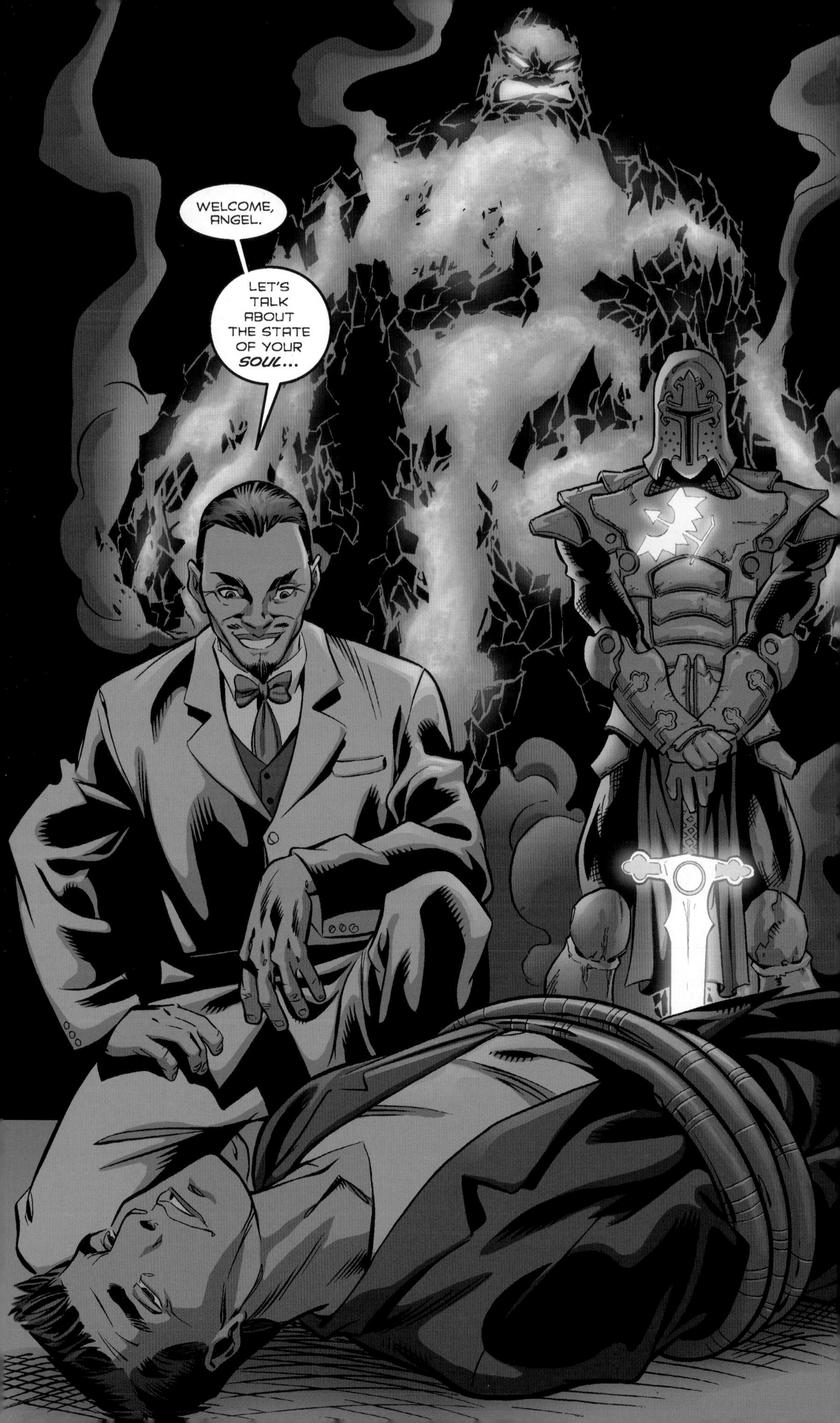
WELCOME, ANGEL.
LET'S TALK ABOUT THE STATE OF YOUR *SOUL*...

Four

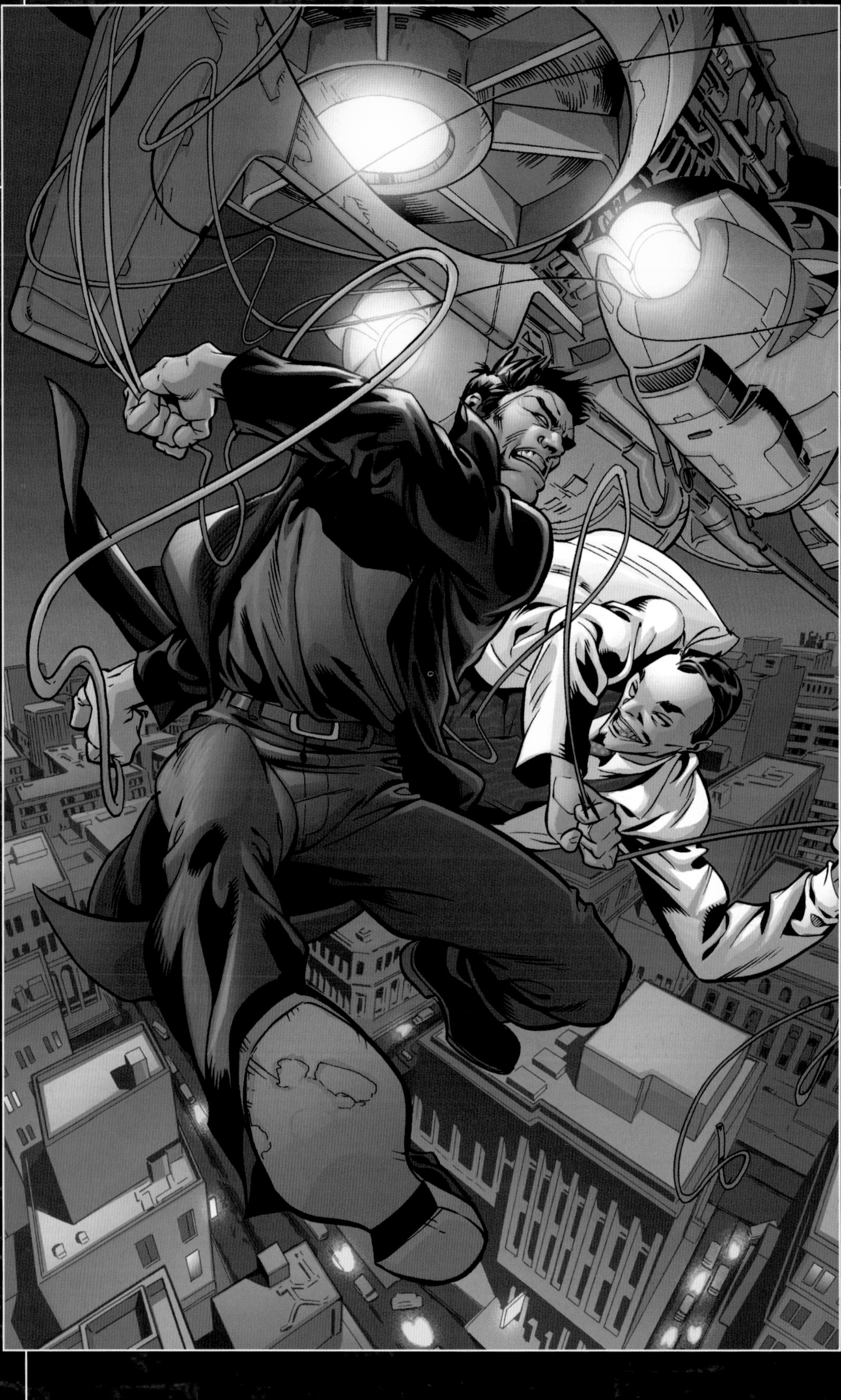

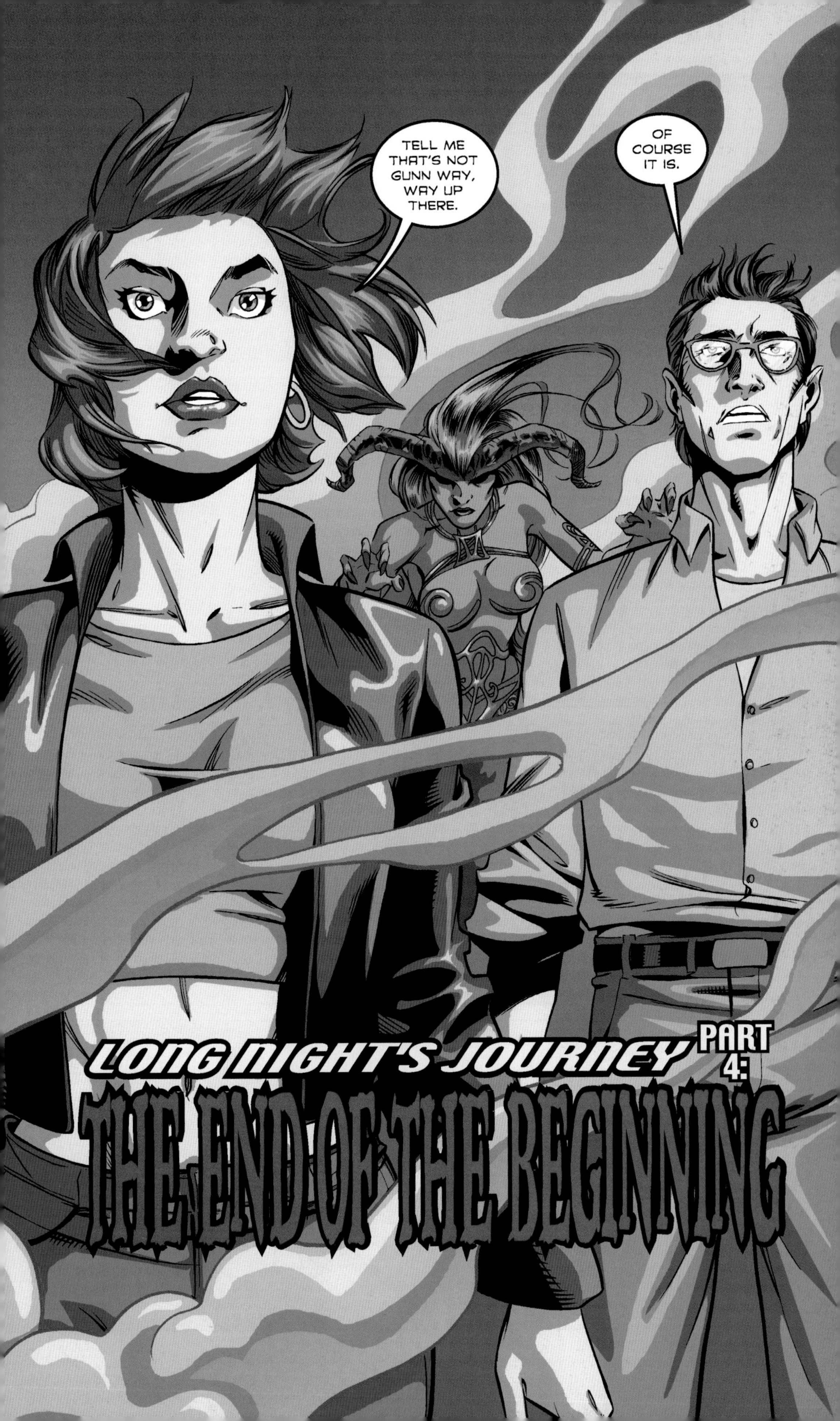

TELL ME THAT'S NOT GUNN WAY, WAY UP THERE.
OF COURSE IT IS.
LONG NIGHT'S JOURNEY PART 4:
THE END OF THE BEGINNING

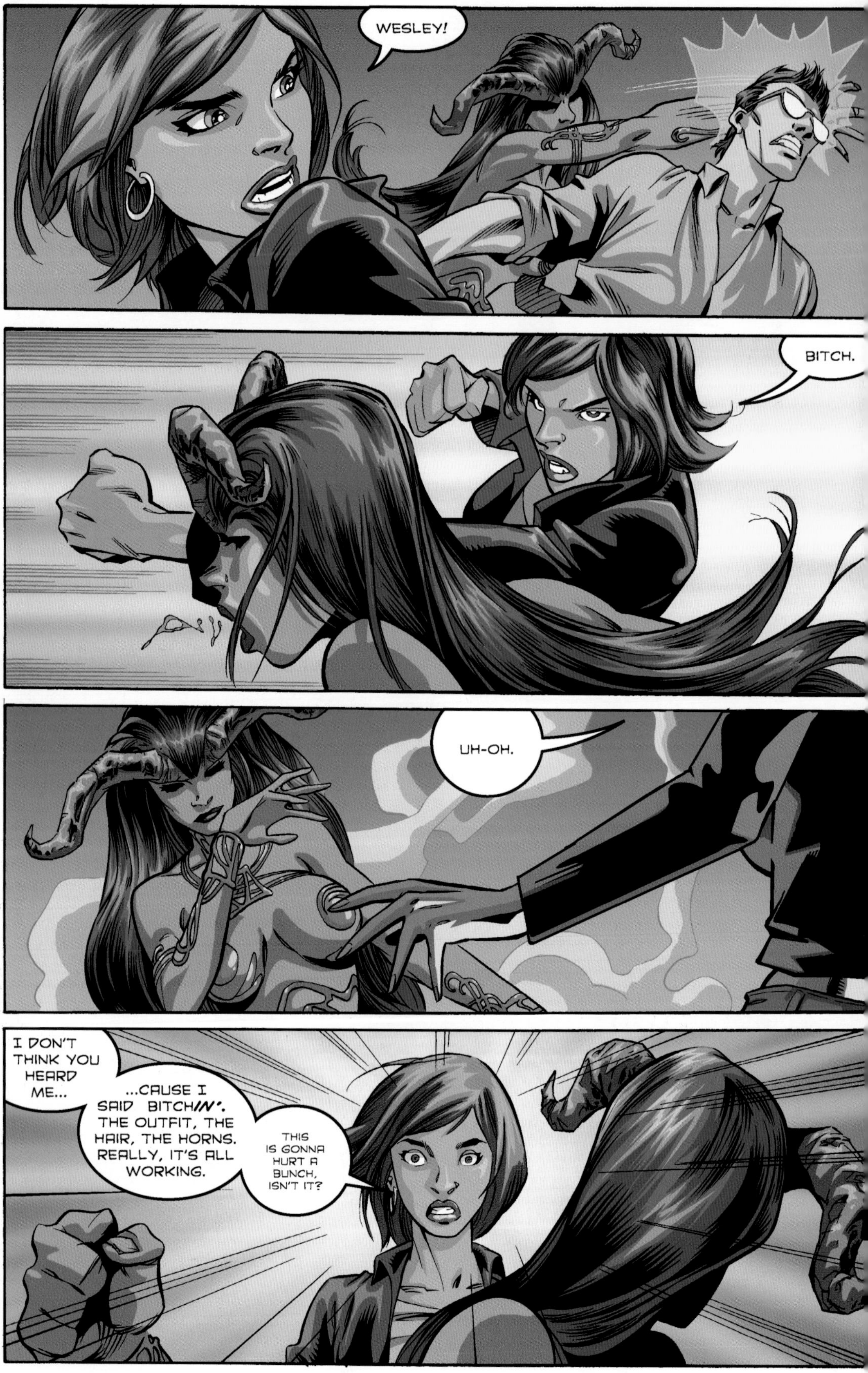

WESLEY!
BITCH.
UH-OH.
I DON'T THINK YOU HEARD ME...
...CAUSE I SAID BITCHIN'. THE OUTFIT, THE HAIR, THE HORNS. REALLY, IT'S ALL WORKING.
THIS IS GONNA HURT A BUNCH, ISN'T IT?

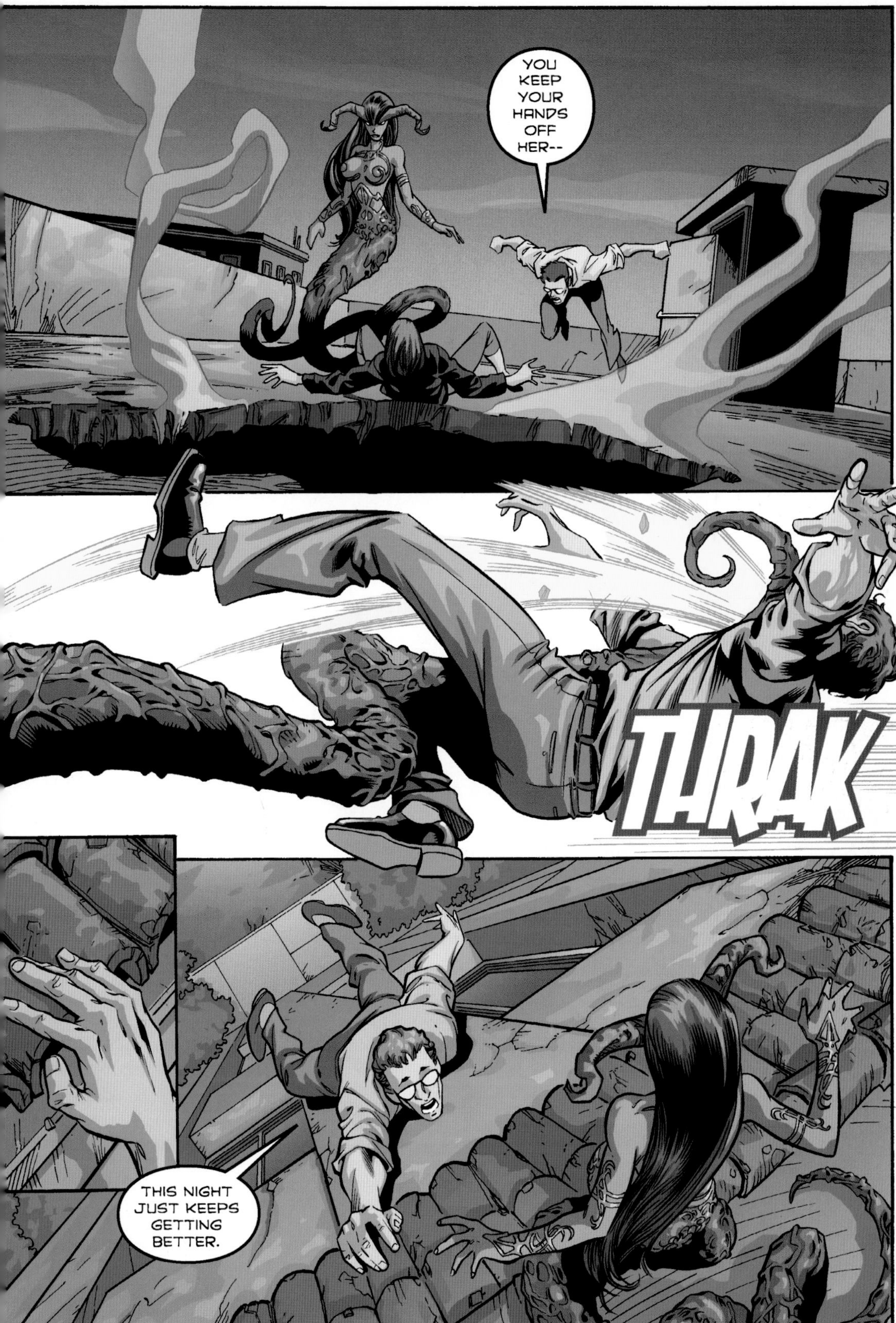
YOU KEEP YOUR HANDS OFF HER--
THRAK
THIS NIGHT JUST KEEPS GETTING BETTER.

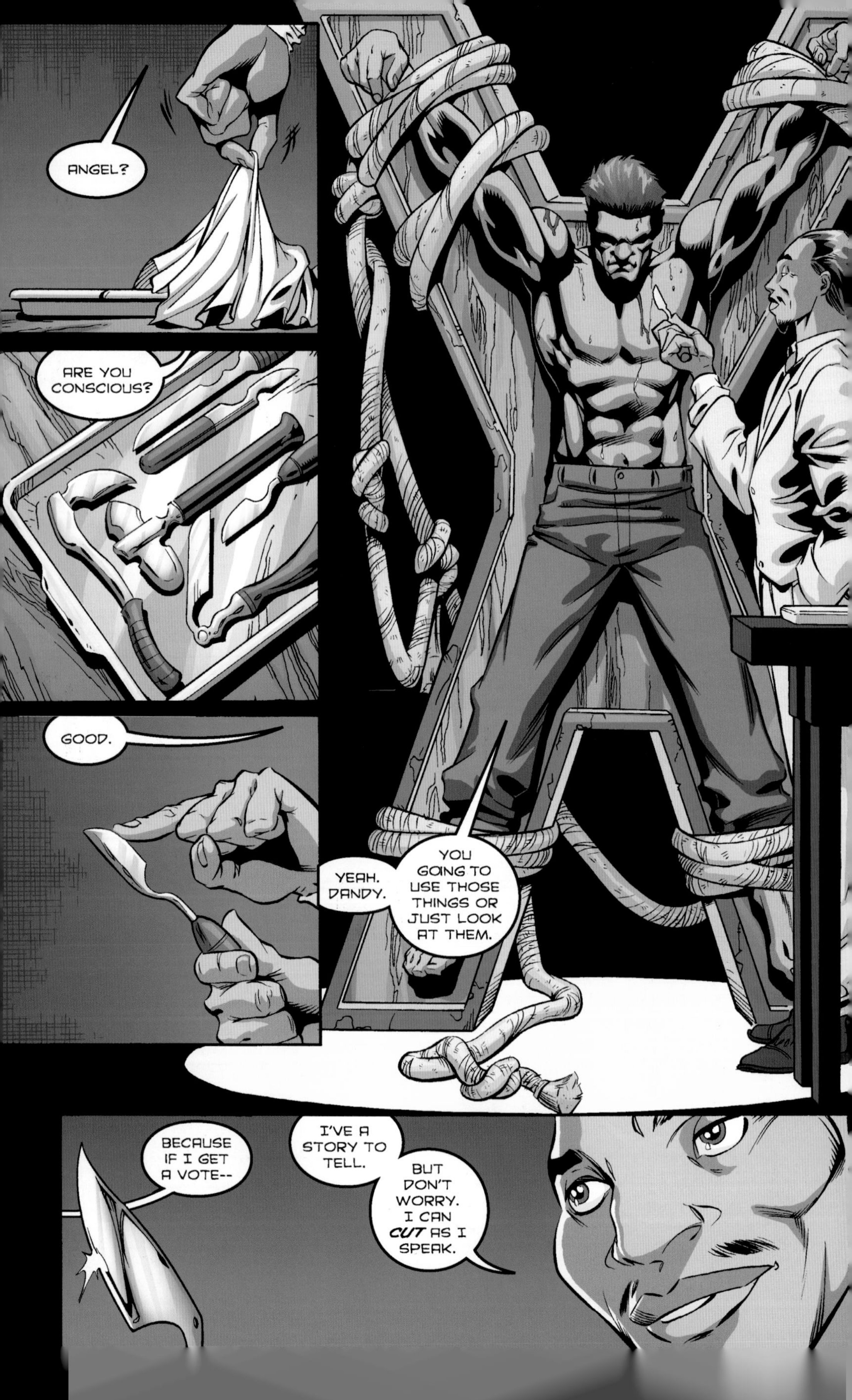

ANGEL?
ARE YOU CONSCIOUS?
GOOD.
YEAH. DANDY.
YOU GOING TO USE THOSE THINGS OR JUST LOOK AT THEM.
BECAUSE IF I GET A VOTE--
I'VE A STORY TO TELL.
BUT DON'T WORRY. I CAN *CUT* AS I SPEAK.

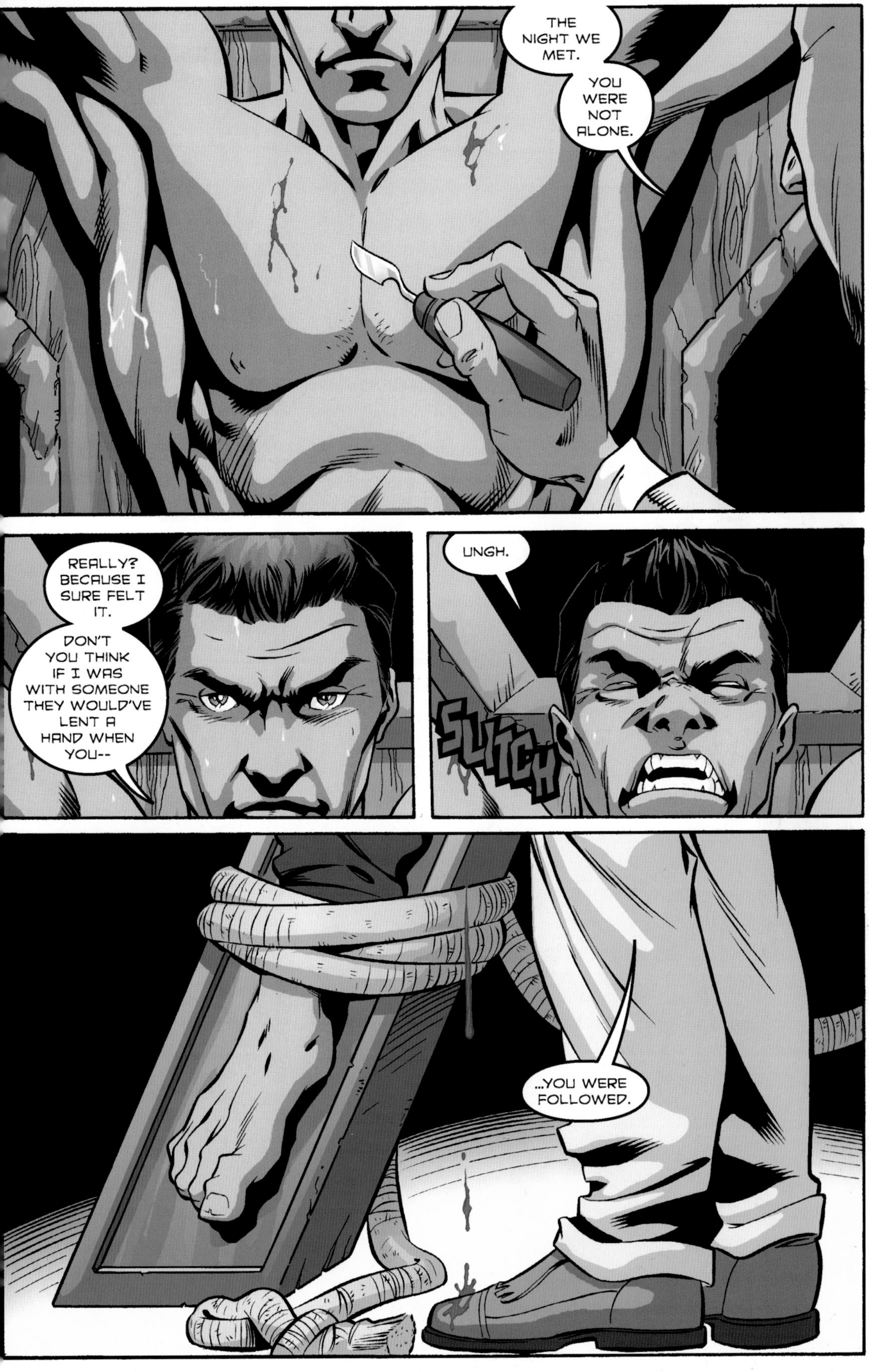
THE NIGHT WE MET.
YOU WERE NOT ALONE.
REALLY? BECAUSE I SURE FELT IT.
DON'T YOU THINK IF I WAS WITH SOMEONE THEY WOULD'VE LENT A HAND WHEN YOU--
UNGH.
SLITCH
...YOU WERE FOLLOWED.

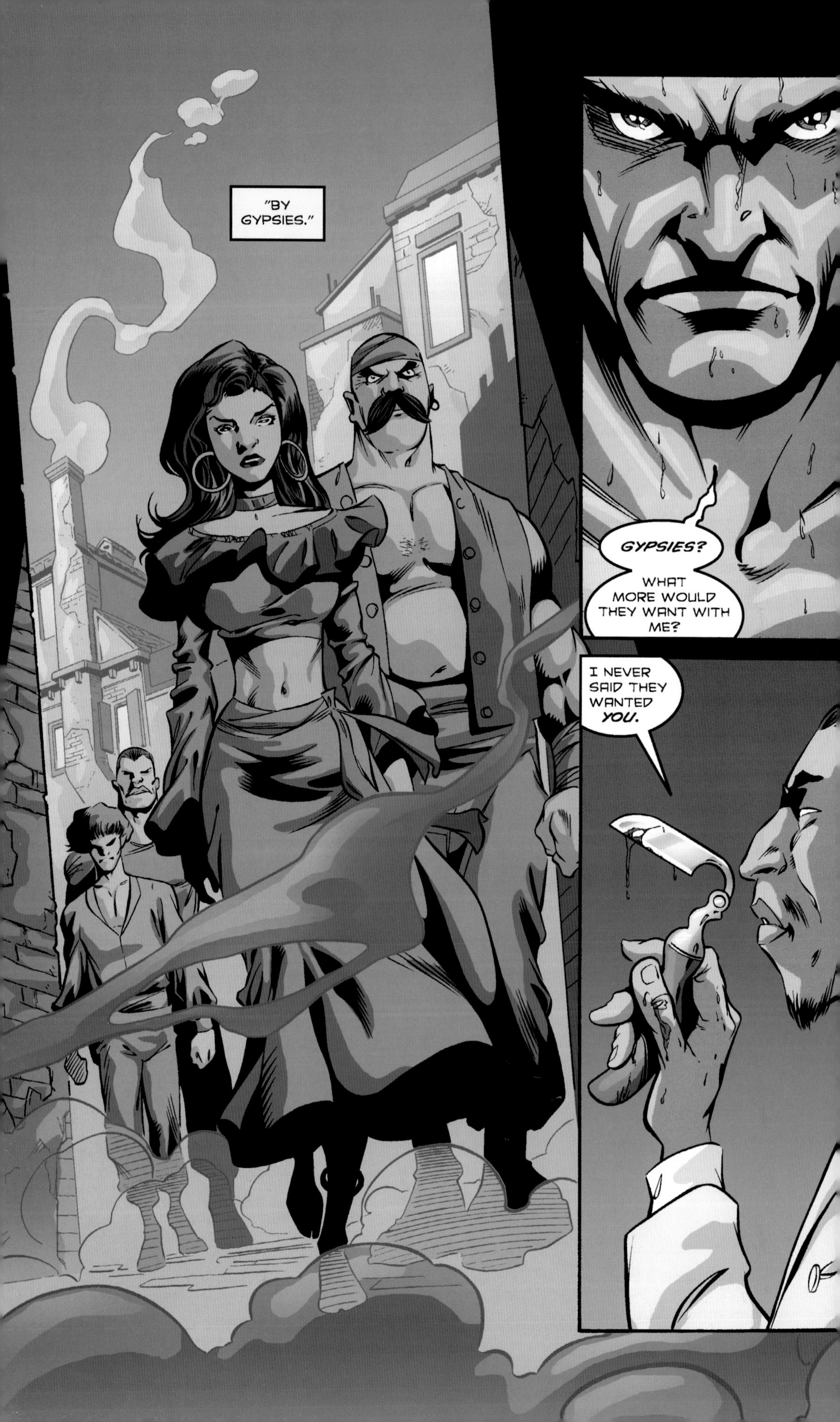
"BY GYPSIES."
GYPSIES?
WHAT MORE WOULD THEY WANT WITH ME?
I NEVER SAID THEY WANTED YOU.

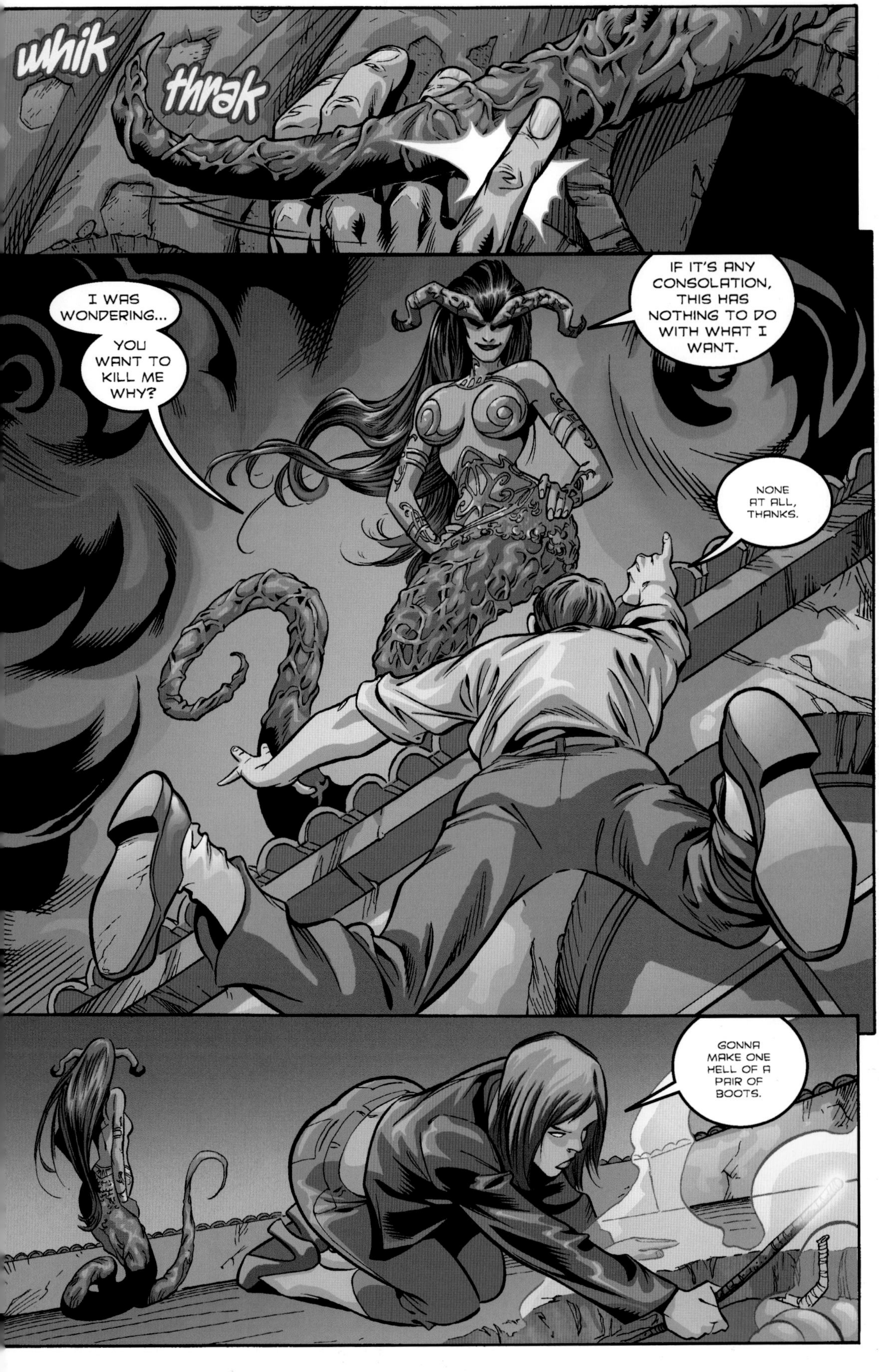
whik
thrak
I WAS WONDERING...
YOU WANT TO KILL ME WHY?
IF IT'S ANY CONSOLATION, THIS HAS NOTHING TO DO WITH WHAT I WANT.
NONE AT ALL, THANKS.
GONNA MAKE ONE HELL OF A PAIR OF BOOTS.

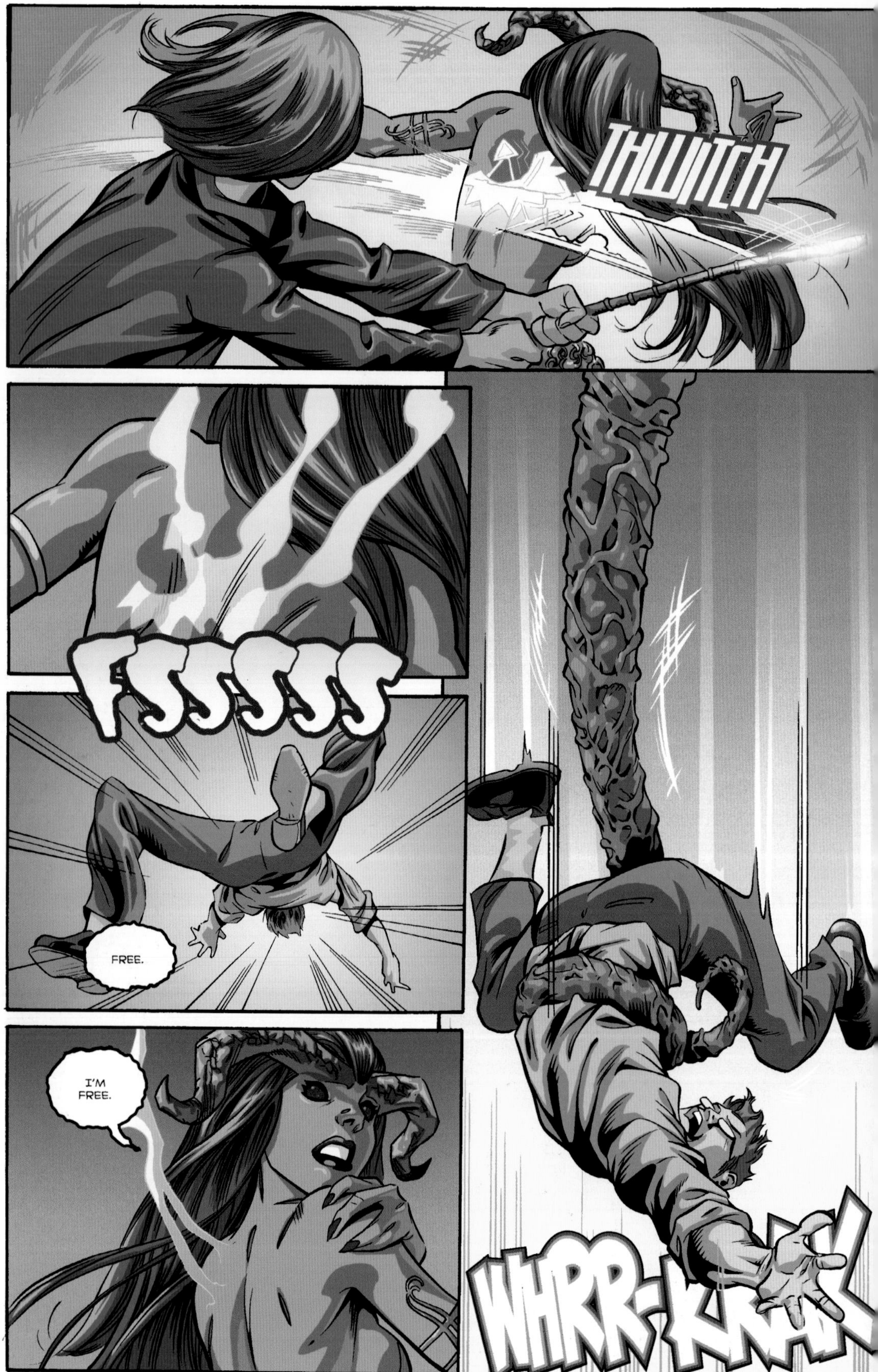
THWITCH
FSSSSS
FREE.
I'M FREE.
WHRR-KRAK

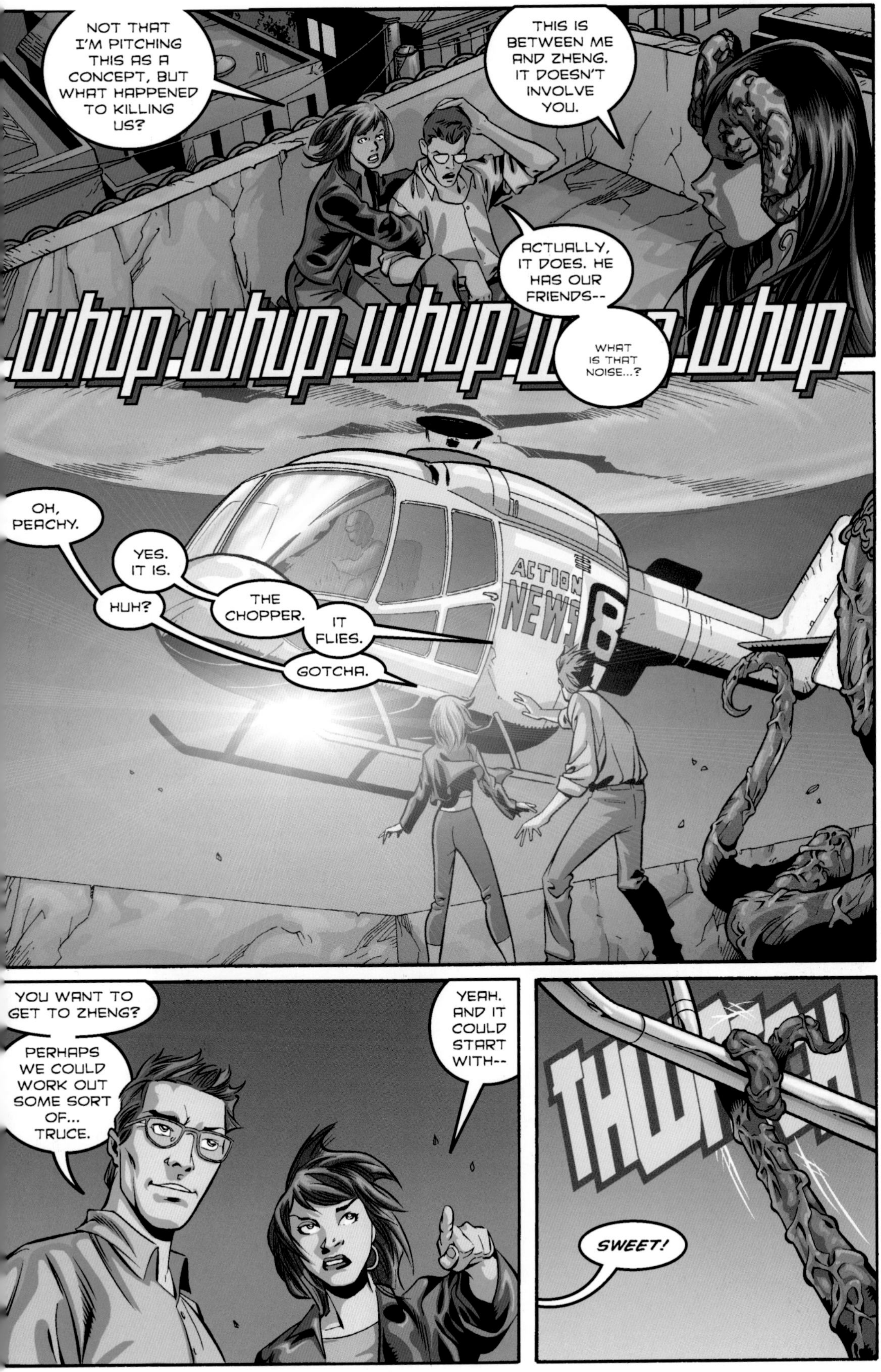
NOT THAT I'M PITCHING THIS AS A CONCEPT, BUT WHAT HAPPENED TO KILLING US?
THIS IS BETWEEN ME AND ZHENG. IT DOESN'T INVOLVE YOU.
ACTUALLY, IT DOES. HE HAS OUR FRIENDS--
WHUP.WHUP.WHUP.
WHUP
WHAT IS THAT NOISE...?
OH, PEACHY.
YES. IT IS.
HUH?
THE CHOPPER.
IT FLIES.
GOTCHA.
ACTION NEWS 8
YOU WANT TO GET TO ZHENG?
PERHAPS WE COULD WORK OUT SOME SORT OF... TRUCE.
YEAH. AND IT COULD START WITH--
SWEET!

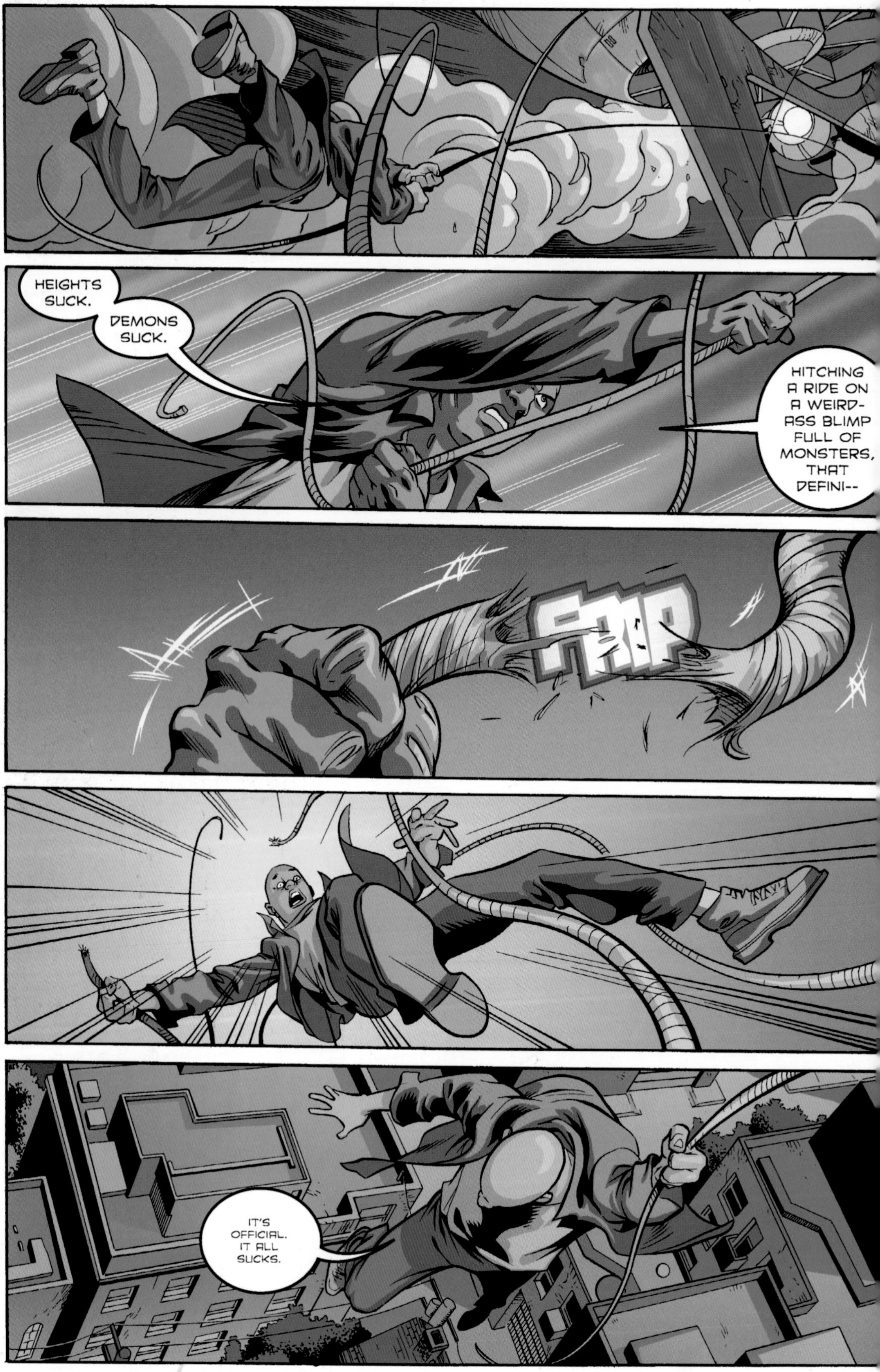
HEIGHTS SUCK.
DEMONS SUCK.
HITCHING A RIDE ON A WEIRD-ASS BLIMP FULL OF MONSTERS, THAT DEFINI--
RRIP
IT'S OFFICIAL. IT ALL SUCKS.

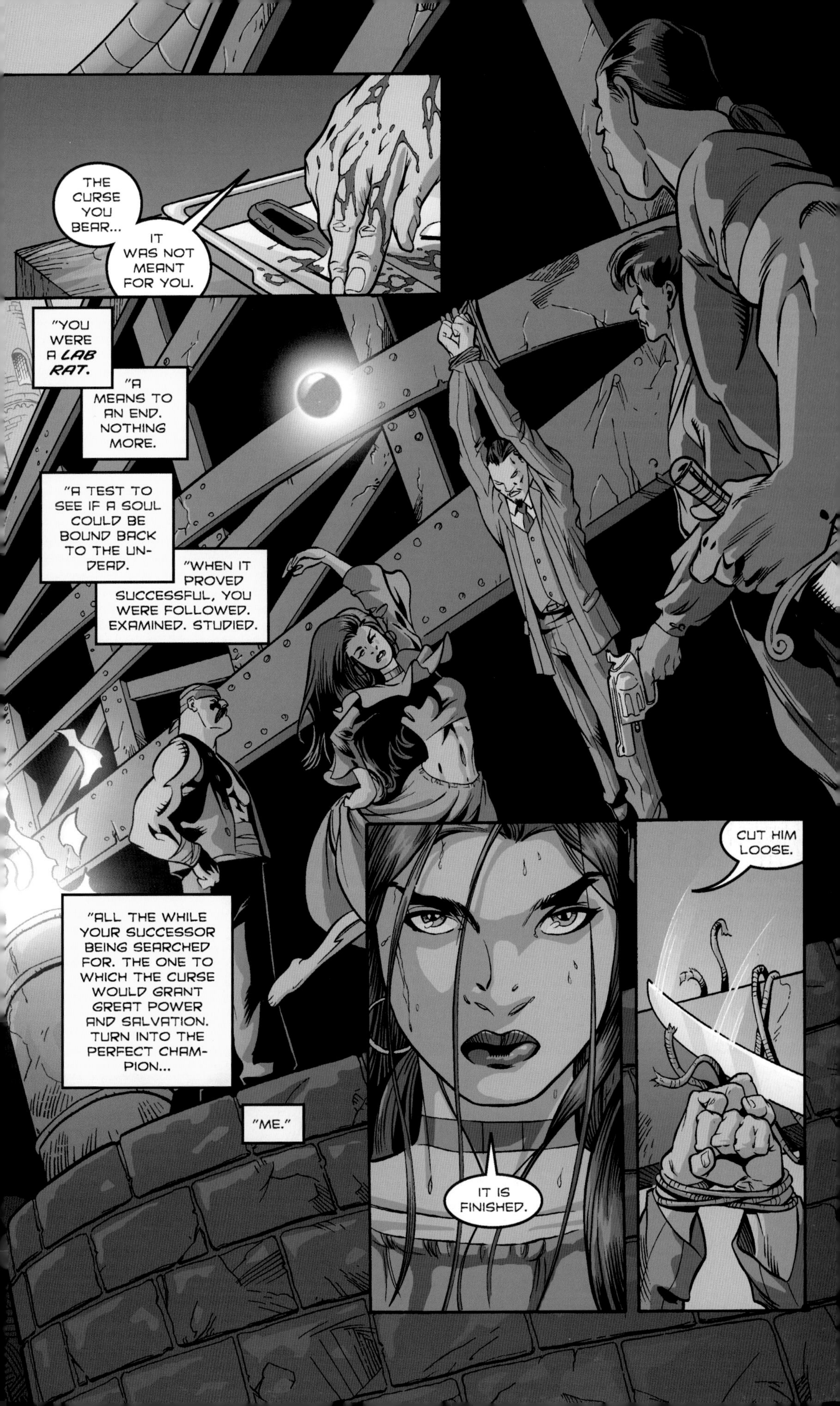

THE CURSE YOU BEAR...
IT WAS NOT MEANT FOR YOU.
"YOU WERE A *LAB RAT*.
"A MEANS TO AN END. NOTHING MORE.
"A TEST TO SEE IF A SOUL COULD BE BOUND BACK TO THE UN-DEAD.
"WHEN IT PROVED SUCCESSFUL, YOU WERE FOLLOWED. EXAMINED. STUDIED.
"ALL THE WHILE YOUR SUCCESSOR BEING SEARCHED FOR. THE ONE TO WHICH THE CURSE WOULD GRANT GREAT POWER AND SALVATION. TURN INTO THE PERFECT CHAMPION...
"ME."
IT IS FINISHED.
CUT HIM LOOSE.

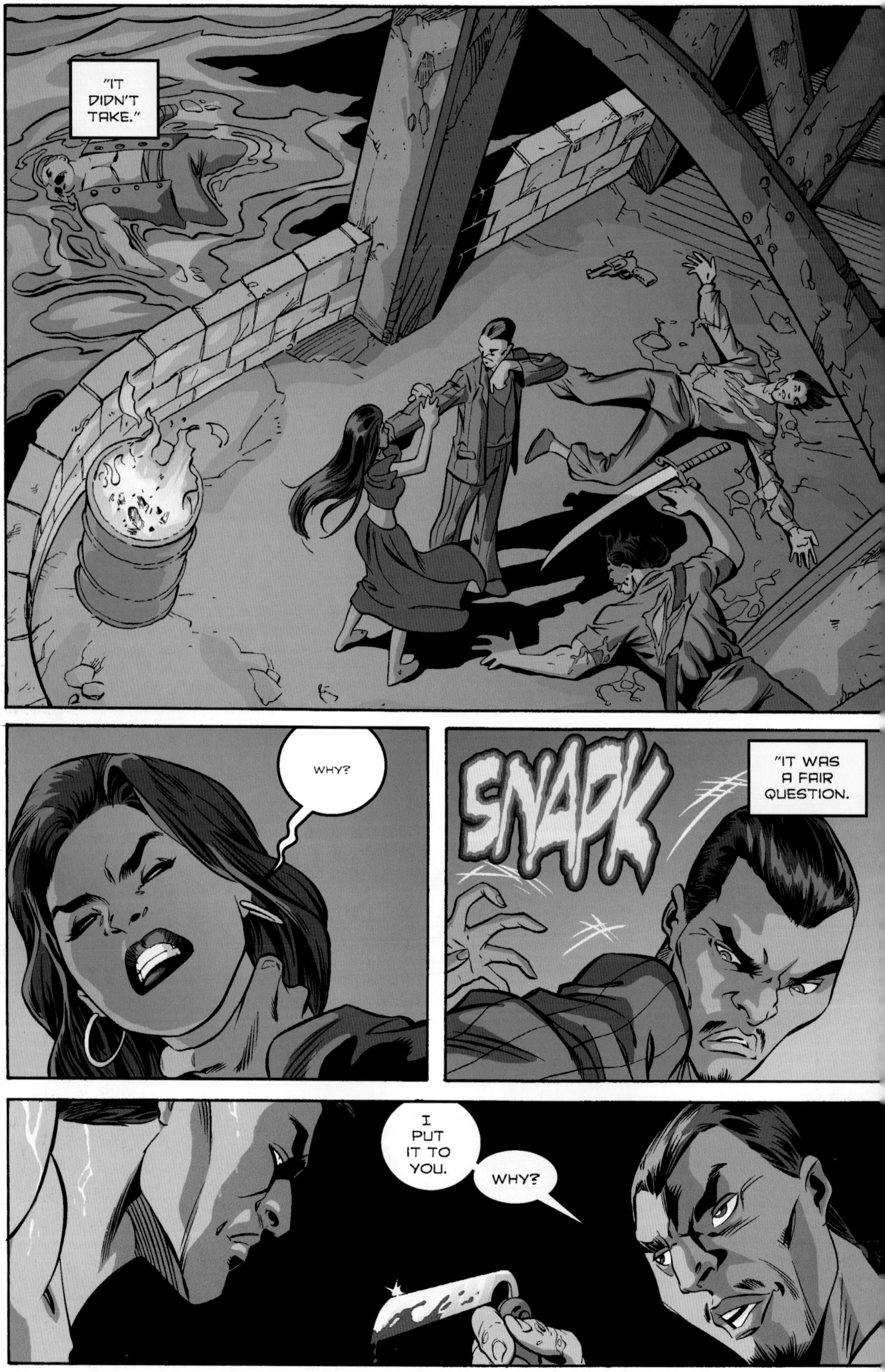
"IT DIDN'T TAKE."
WHY?
SNAPK
"IT WAS A FAIR QUESTION.
I PUT IT TO YOU.
WHY?

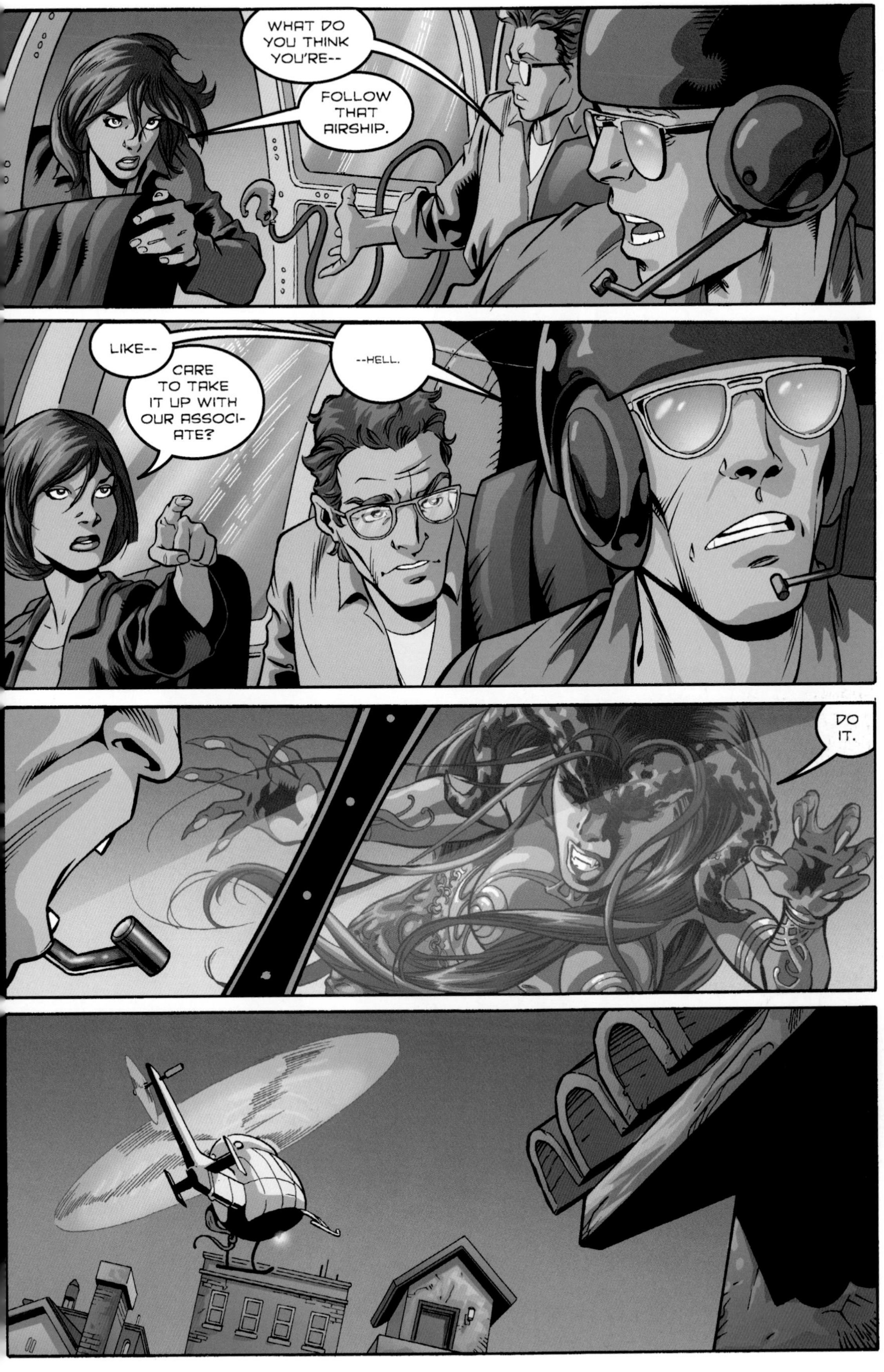
WHAT DO YOU THINK YOU'RE--
FOLLOW THAT AIRSHIP.
LIKE--
CARE TO TAKE IT UP WITH OUR ASSOCI-ATE?
--HELL.
DO IT.

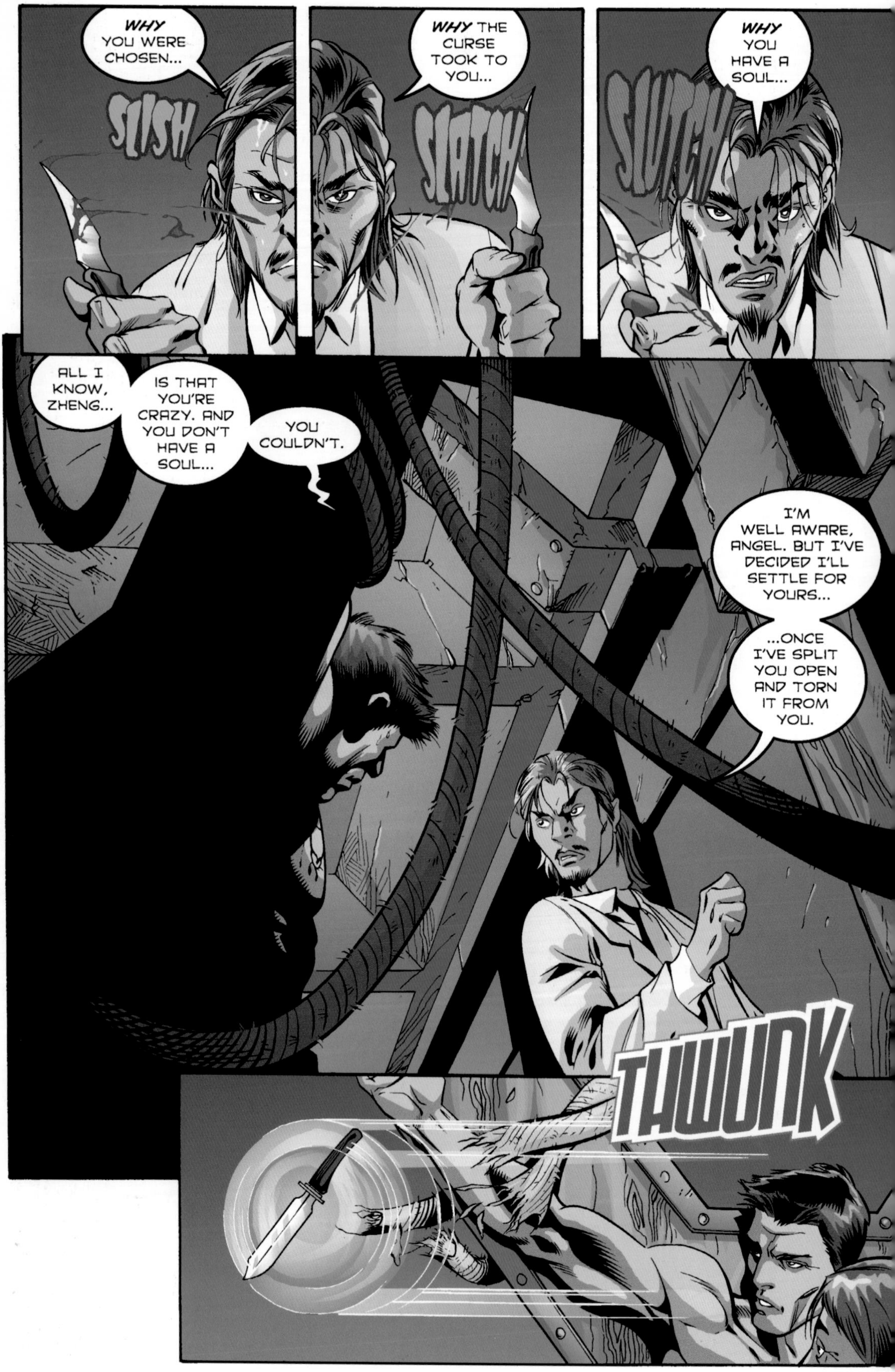

WHY YOU WERE CHOSEN...
SLISH
WHY THE CURSE TOOK TO YOU...
SLATCH
WHY YOU HAVE A SOUL...
SLUTCH
ALL I KNOW, ZHENG...
IS THAT YOU'RE CRAZY. AND YOU DON'T HAVE A SOUL...
YOU COULDN'T.
I'M WELL AWARE, ANGEL. BUT I'VE DECIDED I'LL SETTLE FOR YOURS...
...ONCE I'VE SPLIT YOU OPEN AND TORN IT FROM YOU.
THWUNK

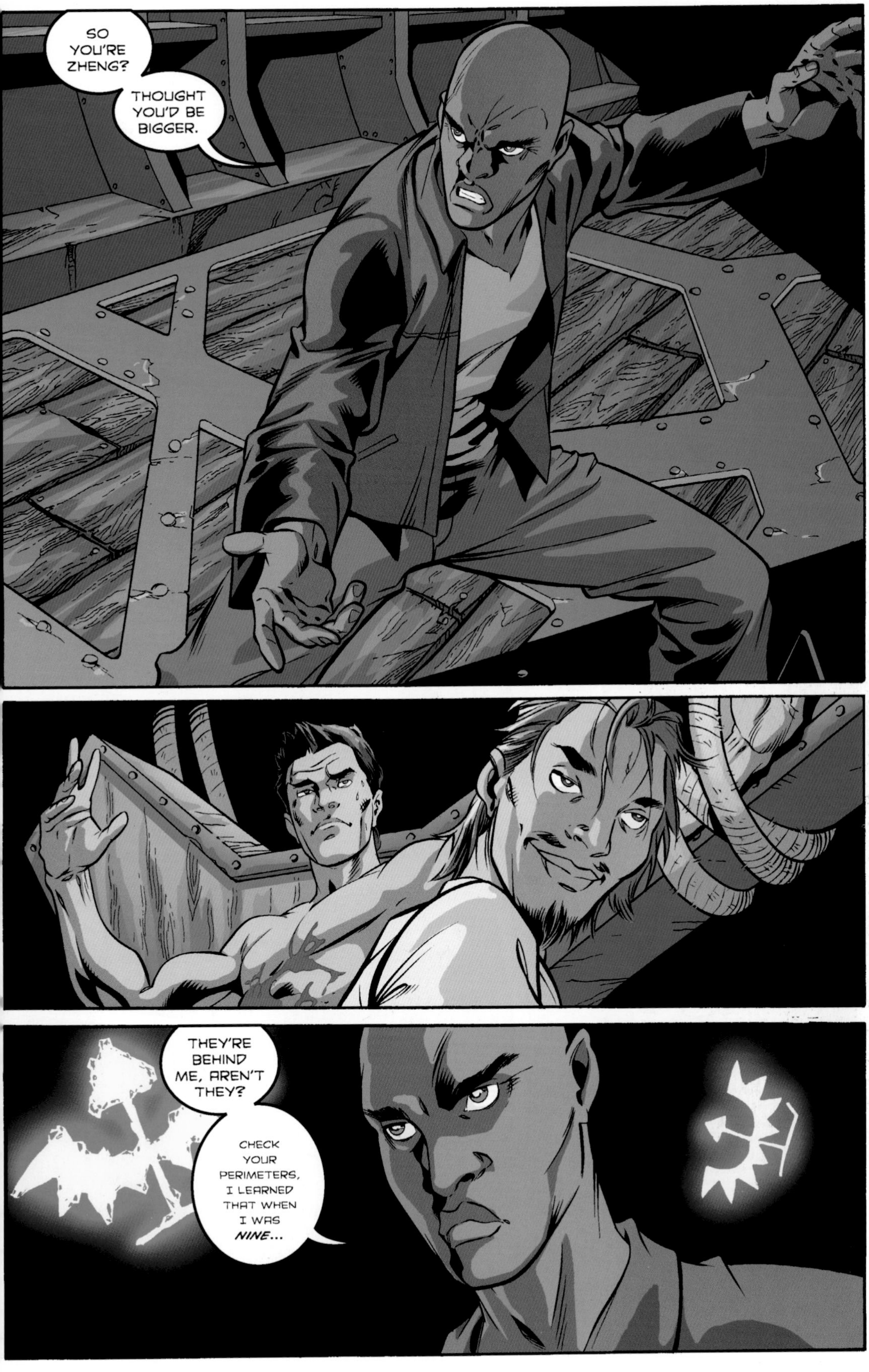
SO YOU'RE ZHENG?
THOUGHT YOU'D BE BIGGER.
THEY'RE BEHIND ME, AREN'T THEY?
CHECK YOUR PERIMETERS, I LEARNED THAT WHEN I WAS *NINE...*

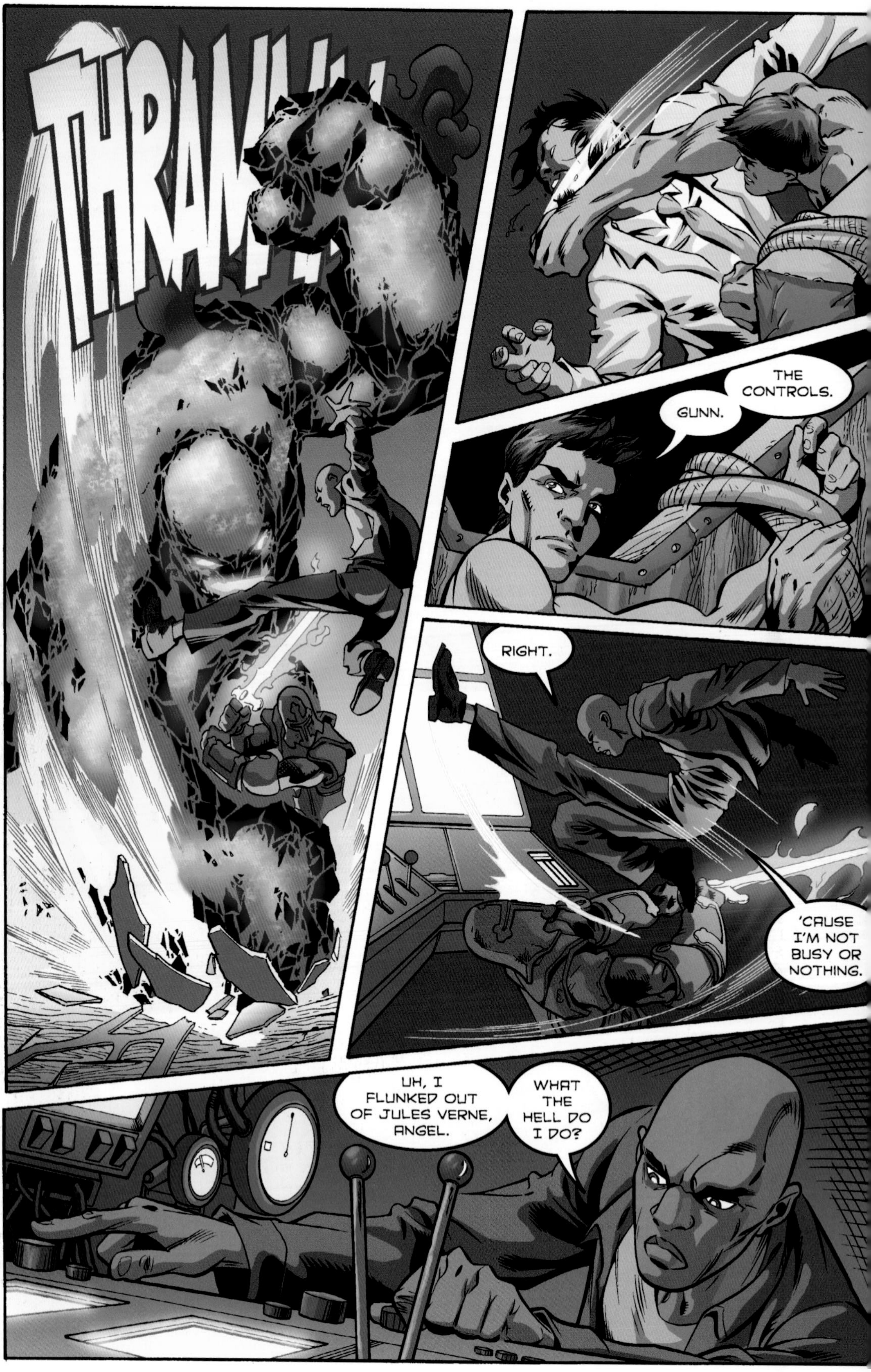
THRAMM!!
GUNN.
THE CONTROLS.
RIGHT.
'CAUSE I'M NOT BUSY OR NOTHING.
UH, I FLUNKED OUT OF JULES VERNE, ANGEL.
WHAT THE HELL DO I DO?

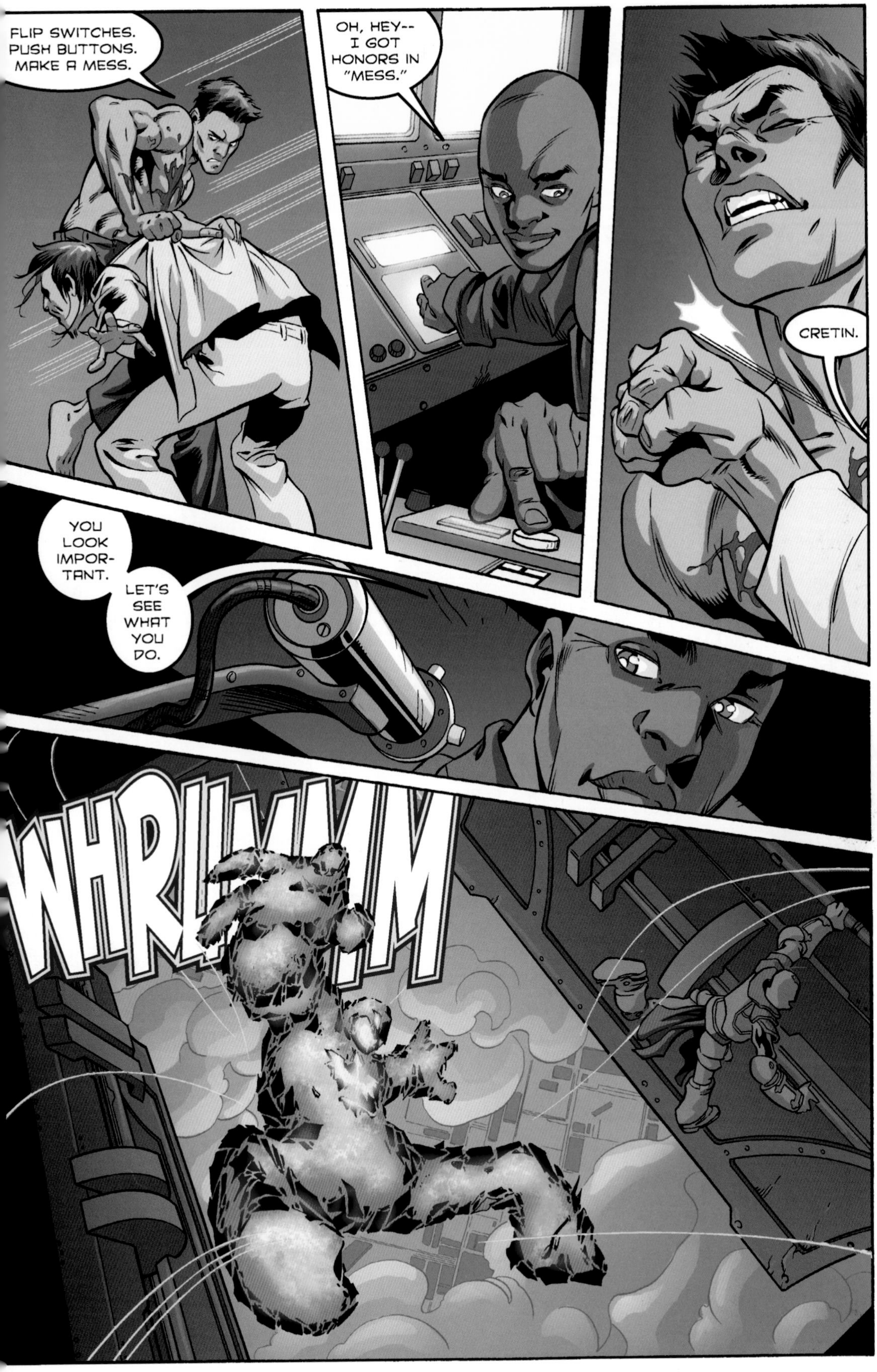
FLIP SWITCHES. PUSH BUTTONS. MAKE A MESS.
OH, HEY-- I GOT HONORS IN "MESS."
CRETIN.
YOU LOOK IMPOR-TANT.
LET'S SEE WHAT YOU DO.
WHRMMM

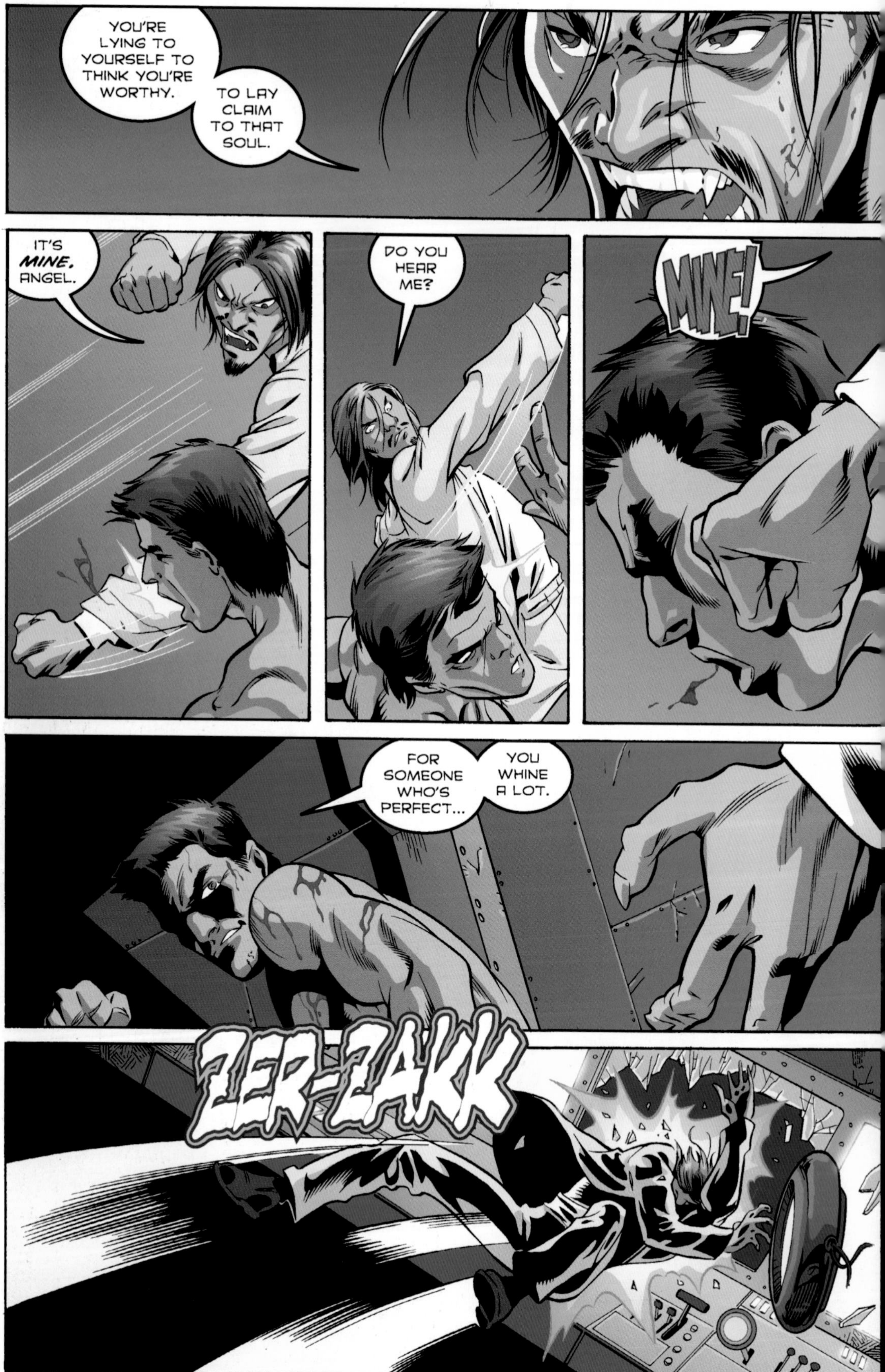
YOU'RE LYING TO YOURSELF TO THINK YOU'RE WORTHY.
TO LAY CLAIM TO THAT SOUL.
IT'S MINE, ANGEL.
DO YOU HEAR ME?
MINE!
FOR SOMEONE WHO'S PERFECT...
YOU WHINE A LOT.
ZER-ZAKK

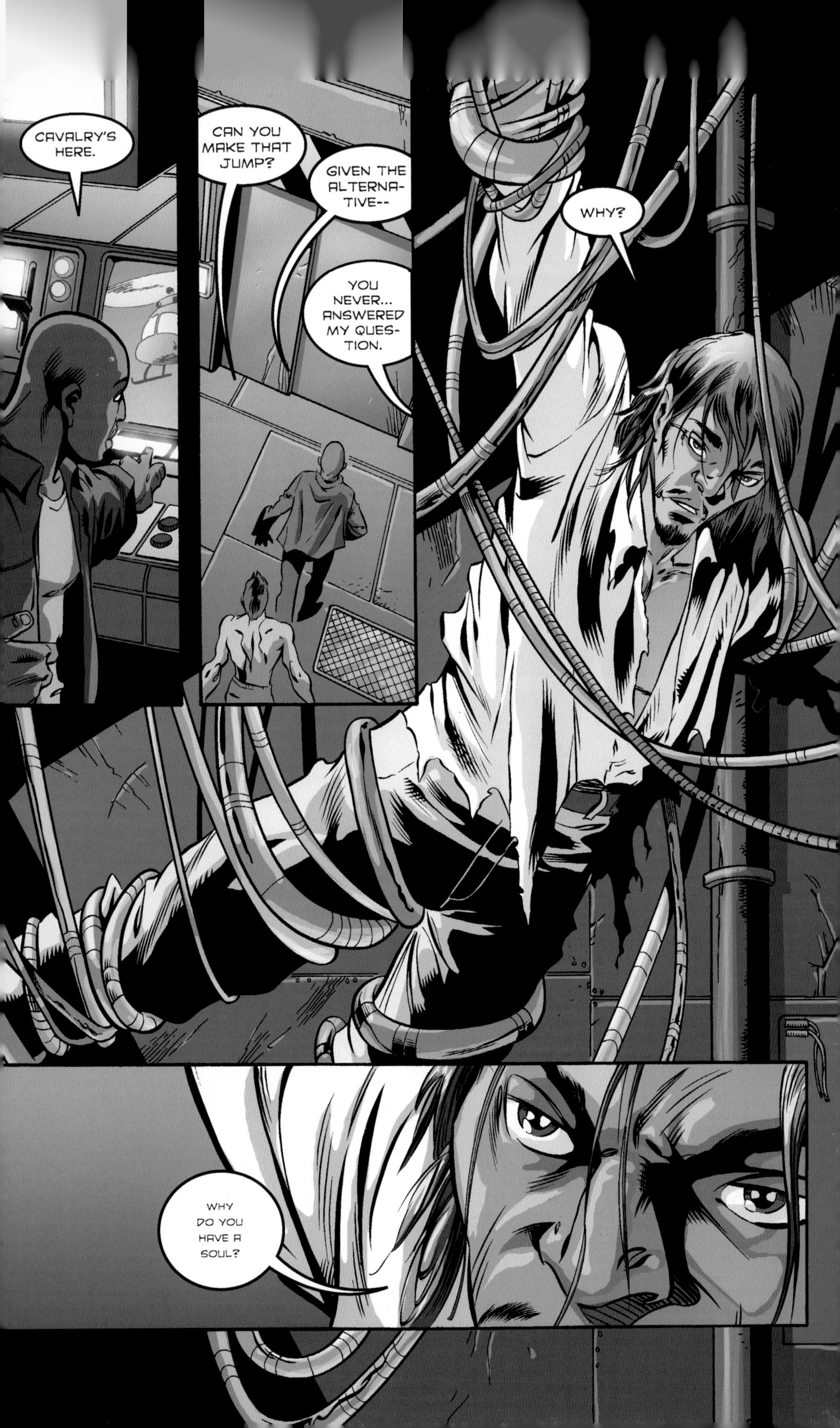
CAVALRY'S HERE.
CAN YOU MAKE THAT JUMP?
GIVEN THE ALTERNATIVE--
YOU NEVER... ANSWERED MY QUESTION.
WHY?
WHY DO YOU HAVE A SOUL?

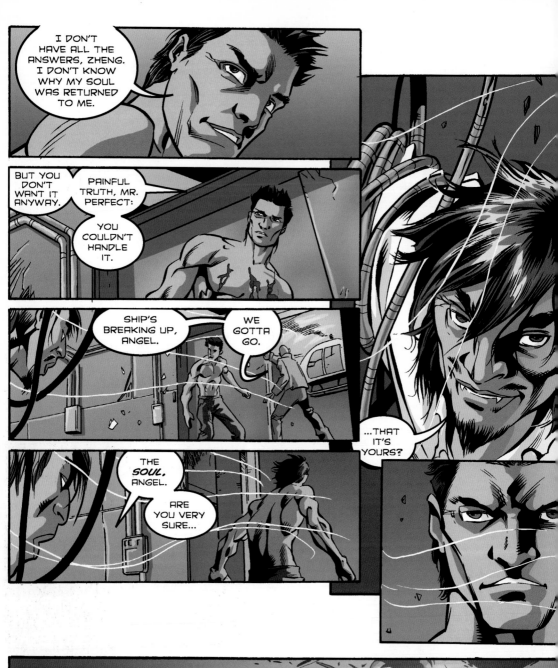

I DON'T HAVE ALL THE ANSWERS, ZHENG. I DON'T KNOW WHY MY SOUL WAS RETURNED TO ME.

BUT YOU DON'T WANT IT ANYWAY.

PAINFUL TRUTH, MR. PERFECT:

YOU COULDN'T HANDLE IT.

SHIP'S BREAKING UP, ANGEL.

WE GOTTA GO.

...THAT IT'S YOURS?

THE SOUL, ANGEL.

ARE YOU VERY SURE...

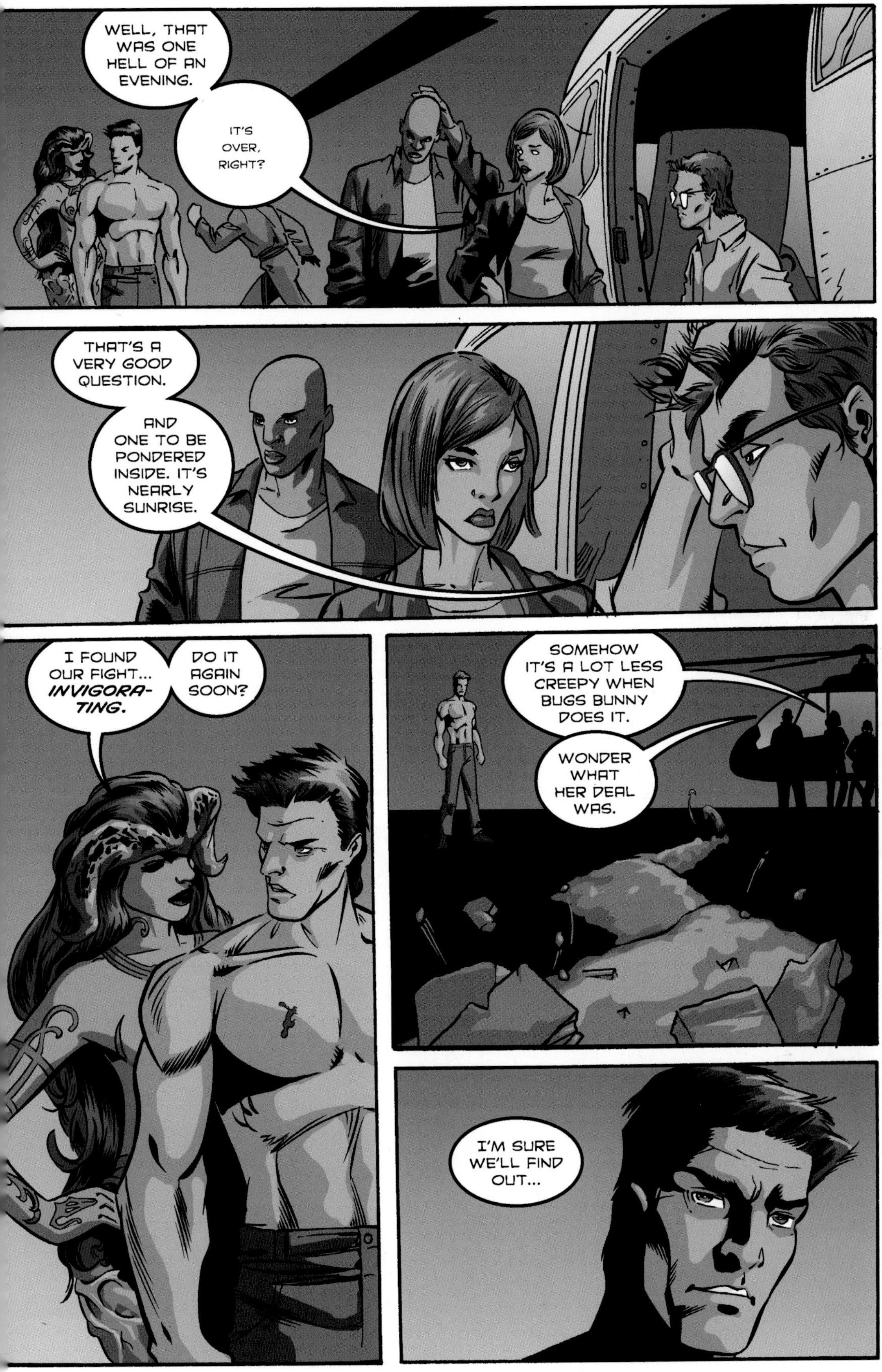
WELL, THAT WAS ONE HELL OF AN EVENING.
IT'S OVER, RIGHT?
THAT'S A VERY GOOD QUESTION.
AND ONE TO BE PONDERED INSIDE. IT'S NEARLY SUNRISE.
I FOUND OUR FIGHT... *INVIGORA-TING.*
DO IT AGAIN SOON?
SOMEHOW IT'S A LOT LESS CREEPY WHEN BUGS BUNNY DOES IT.
WONDER WHAT HER DEAL WAS.
I'M SURE WE'LL FIND OUT...

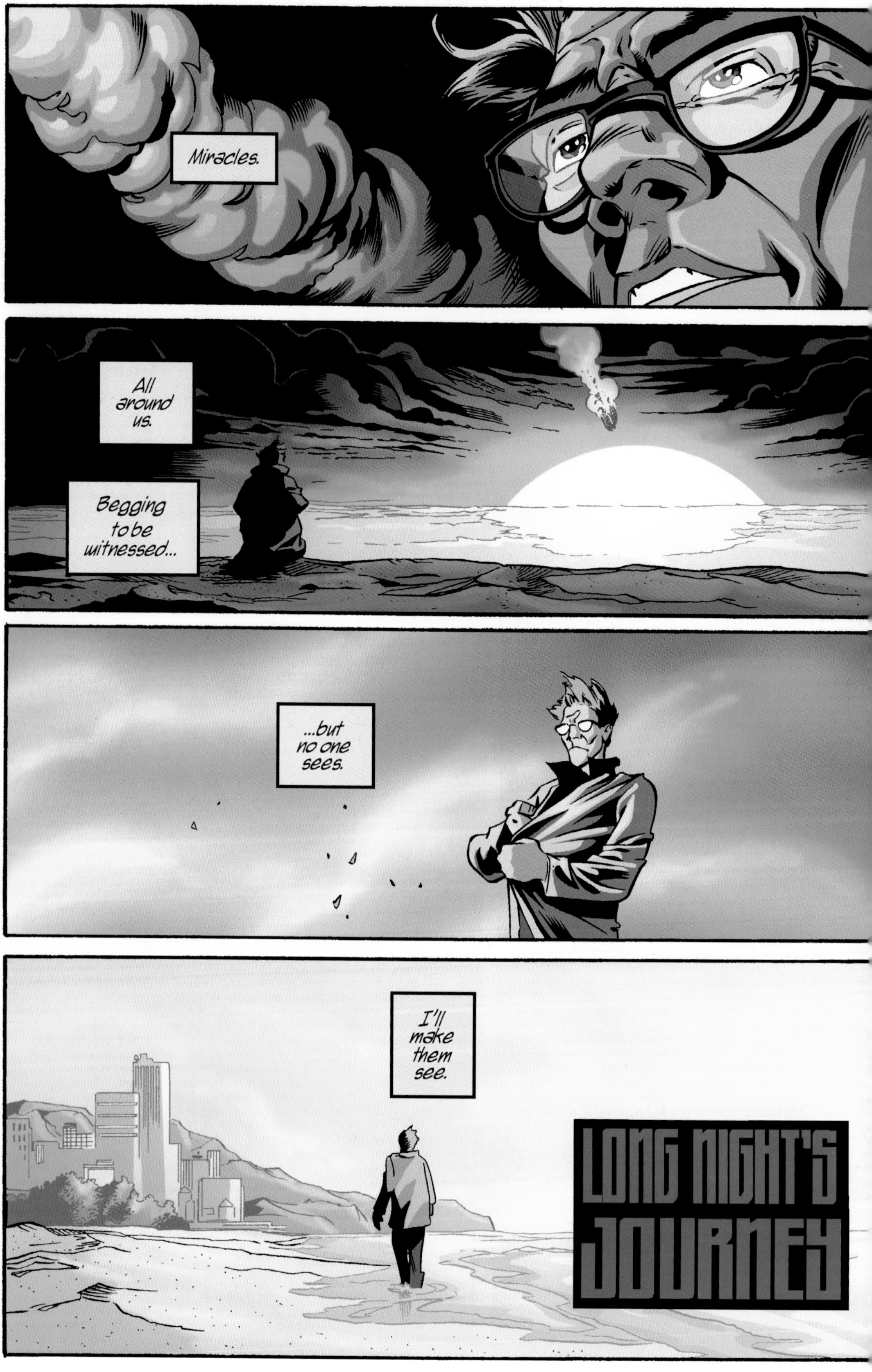
Miracles.
All around us.
Begging to be witnessed...
...but no one sees.
I'll make them see.
LONG NIGHT'S JOURNEY

SKETCHBOOK

by Mel Rubi

Notes by Brett Matthews and Scott Allie

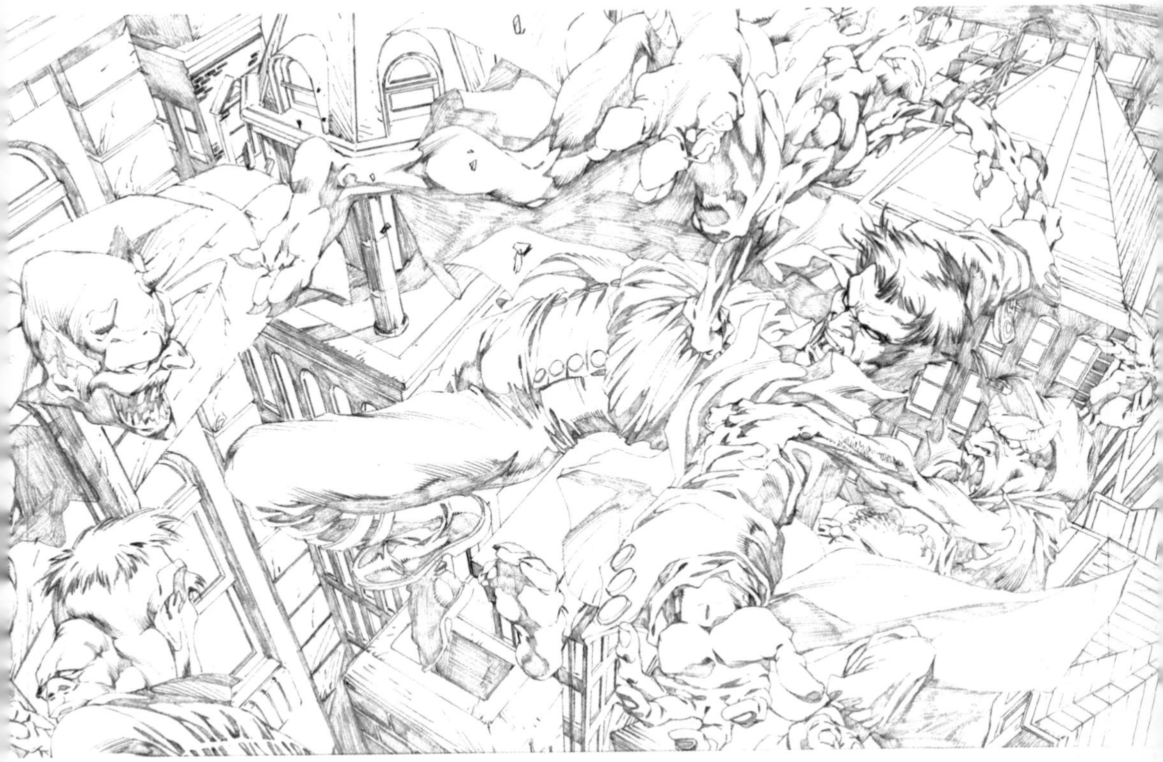

Mel Rubi had tried out for the *Buffy the Vampire Slayer* comic at a time when I didn't need a new artist. I thought he might work better for the darker world of *Angel*. This was right after Joss had told me he wanted to take over *Angel* with a new, more exciting look. So I tried to explain that vision to Mel, and this is what we got.

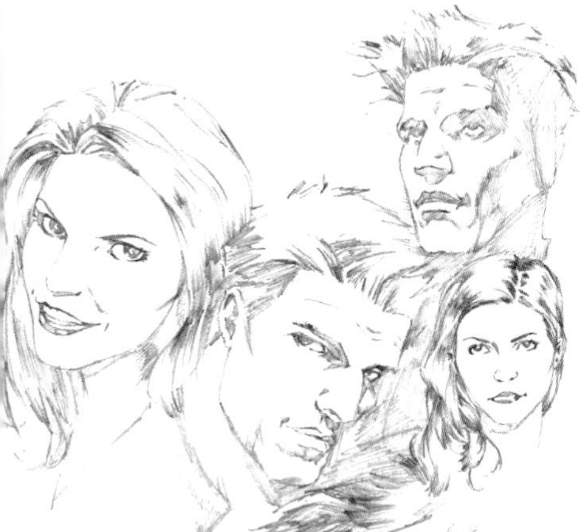

This is definitely the image that got Mel the job. I remember that Joss and I expected a very long and exhaustive search for an interesting artist to help define the book's new, more action-oriented direction.

Then Scott sent us this spread, and we were neither long nor exhausted. We hired him on the spot.

I love this picture. It remains my favorite Angel Mel's ever drawn.

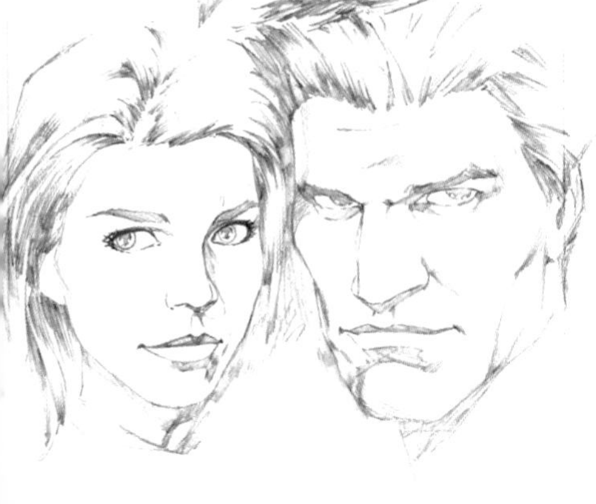

This came with the spread of Angel in action, a quick study of the characters, which I think really does a lot with their personalities.

This is the other piece that got Mel the gig.

I really like his Angel. To me it's just the right combination of actor likeness and artistic license. And he got the hair right. Never underestimate the importance of Angel's hair.

Cordelia has probably changed the most over the course of the first arc. If you leaf back through this volume you hold, you'll notice that Cordy looks quite a bit different between the first and second issue, and from the second to the third. This was a case of telling Mel to let go a little bit, to do a great comic Cordelia instead of being hamstrung trying to pull off exact likenesses on every page. I think this is most clearly seen in issue three, where Mel and the look of the characters really hit their stride.

And I miss the long-haired Cordelia, too.

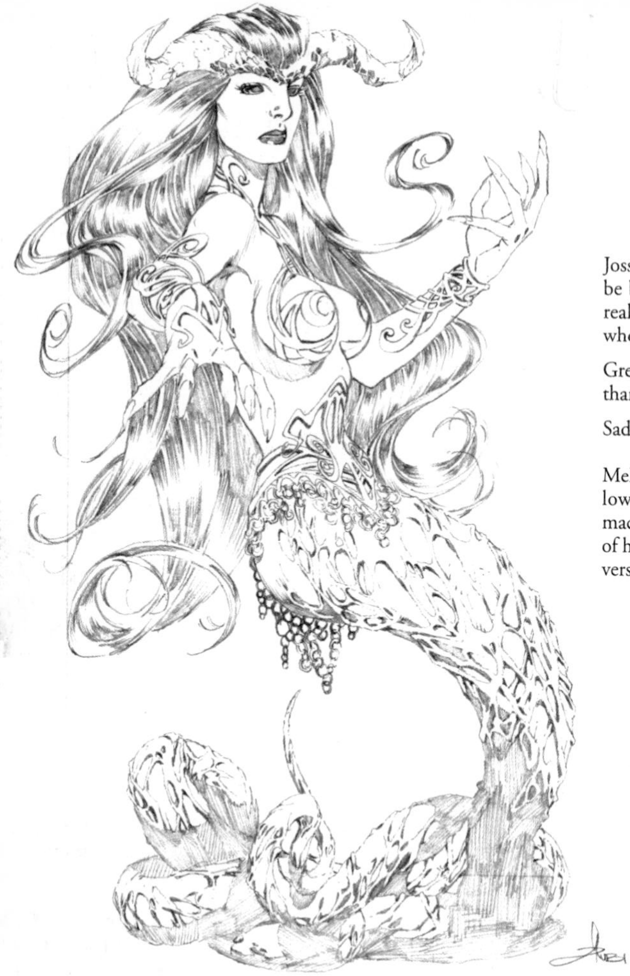

Joss and I originally thought this character was going to be blue, the reason being blue chicks are hot. We soon realized we were maybe the only two guys in the world who held that opinion. So …

Green turned out to be a much better fit for the design than blue.

Sadly.

Mel's original design for the Silthe had this real unique lower body, which didn't make for the best fighting machine. And since that was what she'd be spending a lot of her time doing, Mel streamlined her a little for the final version.

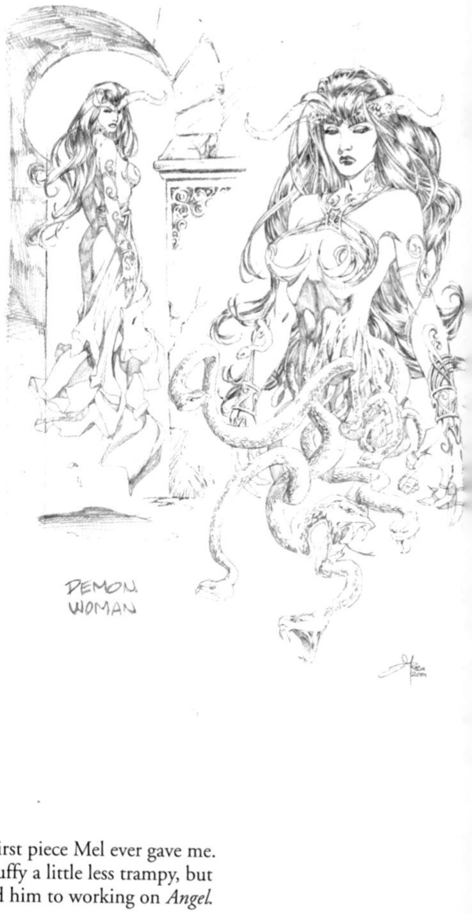
DEMON
WOMAN

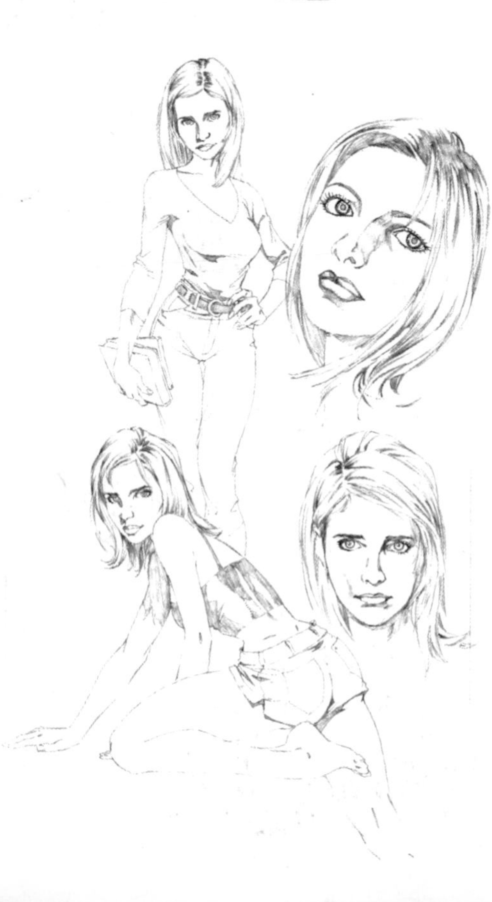

This was the first piece Mel ever gave me. We like our Buffy a little less trampy, but this is what led him to working on *Angel*.

The Kryll.

This design remained completely intact and the characters appear "as is" in issue one. The only difference being that they're dressed in contemporary clothes and driving a DeSoto. How I love comics.

One of Mel's real strengths is his monster designs—that and action scenes. A good combo for this arc.

At the time Mel designed these guys, very early on in the course of the project, I think both he and I expected them to have more of a role in the book. As it is, I think they make a really great looking intro. And for a bit as funny as that emergency-brake sequence, the writers deserved some special monsters to off.

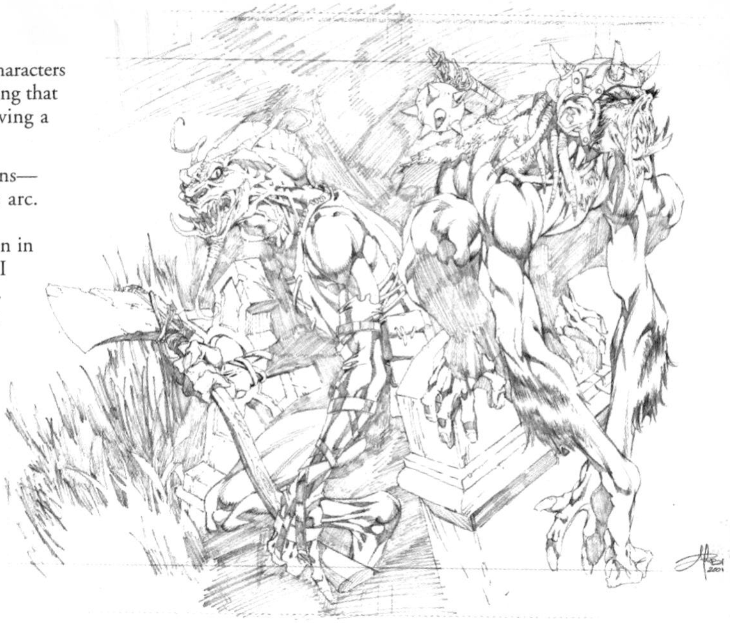

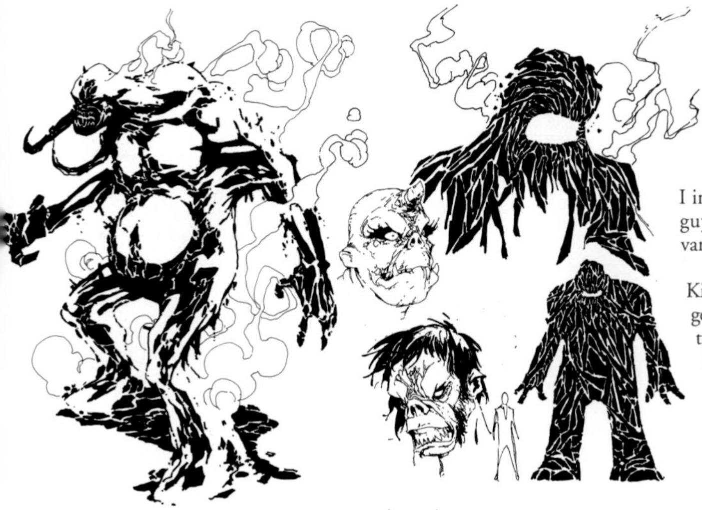

Preliminary sketches for Core.

I immediately liked what Mel came up with for this guy. He had tapped into some pretty interesting variations on a sort of familiar theme.

Kind of shows you how broad this kind of stuff can get, how infinite the possibilities are. We actually chose to combine the two main designs on this page into what eventually became the final design for Core.

Core, as he appears.

I really like this sketch, and, if anything, felt like we lost some of the gangliness of the creature in the actual issues. I love the Kirbyesque feet and don't know if their thickness in relationship to the creature's legs ever really translated.

What I love about the version that made it into the book is the intense mass—any panel you see the thing in, it owns the panel.

I love the little business person about to get melted, too.

God bless Mel Rubi.

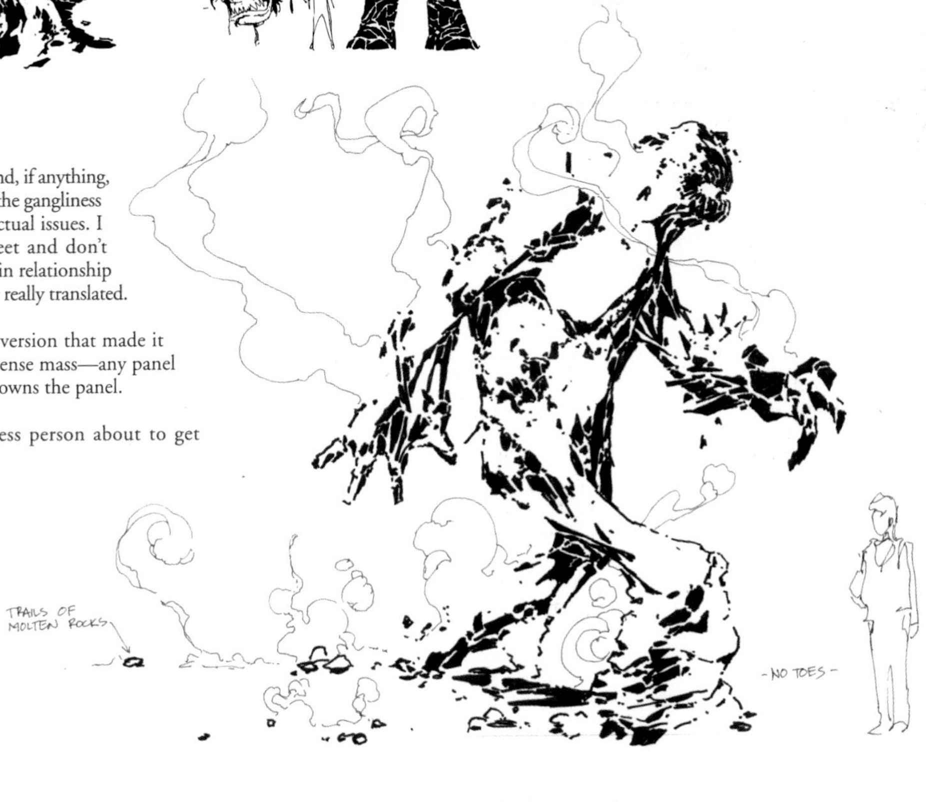
TRAILS OF
MOLTEN ROCKS
-NO TOES-

— Brett Matthews
Los Angeles

— Scott Allie
Portland, Oregon

STAKE OUT THESE ANGEL AND BUFFY THE VAMPIRE SLAYER TRADE PAPERBACKS

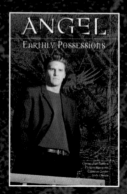

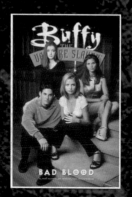